POLITICAL LIFE IN JAPAN

POLITICAL LIFE IN JAPAN

DEMOCRACY IN A REVERSIBLE WORLD

TAKAKO KISHIMA

PRINCETON UNIVERSITY PRESS

PRINCETON, NEW JERSEY

Library of Congress Cataloging-in-Publication Data

Kishima, Takako, 1952–

Political life in Japan : democracy in a reversible world / Takako Kishima.

p.   cm.

Includes bibliographical references (p.) and index.

ISBN 0-691-07895-5 (CL)

1. Japan—Politics and government—1945– 2. Politicians—Japan. 3. Japan—Social

conditions—1945– 4. Marginality, Social—Japan. 5. Political development.

6. Social change. I. Title.

JQ1681.K54   1991

952.04—dc20   91-12805 CIP

Publication of this volume has been assisted by a grant from the Japan
Foundation

This book has been composed in Palatino Typeface

*To My Parents, Kishima Mitsuo and Hideko
and My Sister, Tsubota Noriko*

WITH SOULFUL GRATITUDE

CONTENTS

FIGURES AND TABLES

FIGURES

TABLES

PREFACE

A CHIEF MOTIVATION of this book is to illuminate the lives of ordinary people by focusing on their own worldviews and daily behavior and activities. Although most of the case studies that follow discuss individual political leaders as well as a group of politicians—hardly "ordinary" people—they are treated not as elite policymakers but as ordinary individuals whose daily interactions and relationships happen to be located at the center of politics or as individuals, in some cases, in whom marginality is embodied in certain circumstances. Politicians are the particular focus of this book because people normally see political life as an arena in which deliberate action brings about change—that is, as a setting that exemplifies consciously induced change. Thus it is of special interest to focus on the daily behavior and activities of politicians and the comings and goings in political life more generally that are "nonpolitical" or aesthetic and are shared indiscriminately and ubiquitously by the rest of society. The myriad of ordinary people's seemingly insignificant daily behavior and activities, set apart from those of great leaders or major events and intentional political actions, may, in combinations, have the potential to transform social and political life over time.

Popular notions maintain that social and political change is initiated by elites situated at the center of the system or by social groups intent upon affecting social and political transformations. In other words, people tend to consider power and change without referring to ordinary people's daily behavior and activities. To understand how the latter contribute to the fluidity that allows the possibility of fundamental change from within, it is necessary to rethink the nature of power as well as the nature of change. This approach requires us to incorporate wisdom from a wide range of academic disciplines besides political science—from philosophy, structural anthropology, linguistics, religion, sociology, history, and psychology to art.

This challenge is addressed in the present study. First, by taking account of insights found in structuralism, poststructuralism, phenomenology, and symbolic anthropology, I give fresh consideration to the nature of power itself. Then, once I establish that the worldview all human beings have is indispensable for the discussion of power—that is, an ordinary person's power—I conceptualize a new three-dimensional worldview. The three dimensions consist of *nomos*, which comprises the rules, laws, and institutions of society; *cosmos*, whose symbolic order gives nomos meaning; and *chaos*, wherein all meaning and connectedness are lost. Nomos, cosmos, and chaos embody mutually contrasting principles. Each domain is defined always in relation to the other two. Nomos as structure, that is, a network of roles and statuses, is defined by nonstructure, chaos, as well as by another structure, cosmos, as Ueno (1977, 109) discerns. A fragile and constantly shifting balance of force is maintained among these three dynamically related domains.

The key to this three-dimensional worldview is its incorporation of the marginal/liminal domain that lies on the margin and in the interstices of nomos and thereby mediates between cosmos and nomos and between nomos and chaos. A marginal/liminal domain is a symbolic sphere in which the flow of ordinary time is halted and the utilitarian, norm-governed nomos is overpowered. Various forms of marginal beings and liminal states are found in this sphere, and they inherently either have multiple identities or totally lack identity. That is, they may embody mutually contradictory values and characteristics, partially or in full, of two or more disparate domains to which they belong at the same time, or they may lack any identity.

Consequently, they may be destructive as well as creative, for instance, or pure as well as impure. Intrusions of the liminal sphere into ordinary life in nomos occurs through the mediation of these marginal beings and liminal states. They inevitably and ubiquitously cause internal inconsistencies and ambiguities in nomos by bringing in contradictory and incompatible elements from other domains. Nomos constantly needs to have consistency and meaningfulness restored under a new organizational principle that incorporates as well as accommodates both new and old elements.

The unsettling and fluid condition that accompanies this process cannot help but activate ordinary people's reflexivity—that is, their ability to reexamine and comment on anything, including self, that is taken for granted. Everything in nomos may appear to ordinary people to be arbitrary and subject to questioning, including their analyses of themselves, their relationships with others, and the entire system of which they are a part. In other words, with activated reflexivity, people are able to keep themselves from being completely reified with the existing order, authorities, and institutional arrangements. Thus, the possibility of genuine social change that involves all three domains, rather than a change only within nomos, is made available.

Marginal beings and liminal states are crucial to people. Their intrusions into nomos invoke ordinary people's potential and liability to become marginal beings and enter liminal states themselves. In their daily lives, ordinary people constantly experience moments in which they become marginal beings or enter liminal states, ranging from seemingly trivial activities like laughing, daydreaming, dancing, getting drunk, or being absorbed in a movie and play to extraordinary activities such as war, natural disaster, death of a close family member, and a journey to a foreign land. Through such liminal experiences, which take them out of nomos temporally and spatially, ordinary people themselves function as marginal beings, rousing and activating their reflexivity. This activated reflexivity is the core of power of any human being because it prevents the individual from reifying fixed beliefs, ideologies, and values and thereby enable the individual soul to resist domination of any kind at the fundamental level, whether political, religious, or intellectual. Liminal experiences also offer ordinary people qualitatively distinct settings or moments in which they cease to be an aggregate of fragmented roles and statuses. Such moments build spontaneous, egalitarian whole-human-to-whole-human relationships between and among people. The creation of these kinds of bonds of immediacy and intimacy not only prevents the reification process from going forward but possibly affects relationships, social arrangements, and values prevailing in nomos in such a way that they eventually appear to allow flexible management.

It is, therefore, both meaningful and necessary to examine people's behavior and activities in daily life with particular attention to how they are filled spatially and temporally with manifestations of liminality. For the most part, the samples for this study are set in contemporary Japan, but they could have been selected from any society or political system in any period in history. Japanese society is selected because its uniqueness is often asserted in social science literature. On the one hand, Japan is considered to be a modern society that may be comfortably compared with the industrially advanced societies of Western Europe and the United States. On the other hand, Japan is regarded as profoundly unlike the latter because, among other things, even modern urban Japanese life is infinitely rich in ritual symbolism that is scientifically and rationally inexplicable (Barthes 1982, Ohnuki-Tierney 1984). Certainly, Japanese life provides abundant materials for this study. Chosen for the case studies from the vast range of such marginal beings and liminal states in Japanese cultural context are laughter, play, tears, legislators' get-together activities, a blood-oath ritual of a group of young politicians, an orgiastic election campaign, and three politicians who either embodied marginal qualities or manifested liminality under certain circumstances at certain times. Individually, these marginal beings and liminal states may look insignificant. Cumulatively, however, they represent a vast stream of activity operating in myriad ways in ordinary people's lives. Collectively, as in the following case studies, they have the potential to allow genuine change over time in society and politics through their inherently dereifying function.

Besides seemingly trivial daily behavior and activities, any political movements, including revolutionary movements, war, and other major political phenomena, will be more comprehensively grasped when nomos, cosmos, and chaos are seen in intricate relation with one another. Experiences when people become marginal beings or enter liminal states are basic to political life. They are on parade in the myriad rituals and ecstatic moments of political campaigning and electoral politics. They prevail in moments of national tragedy (the *Challenger* explosion and the San Francisco earthquake), fear (the Cuban missile crisis), political scandal (the Lockheed and Recruit scandals in Japan, Watergate and Irangate in the United States), mourning (in the complex reactions to the assassination of President John F. Kennedy in America, and the death of Emperor Showa in Japan), or ecstatic joy (as shown by the German people when the Berlin Wall was finally torn down).

These experiences of daily political life not only help people transcend the rules and structures of society but also activate their reflexivity. In the chapters that follow I intend to focus on these minor intrusions of liminal experiences into the order of the everyday world, which, no matter how insignificant they may appear, ceaselessly threaten to undo that order with their inherently dereifying function. That is, I will focus on cultural particularities on the basis of my conviction, which is shared by an increasing number of scholars, including poststructuralists, that cumulation of trivial, apolitical changes in meaning and material conditions experienced by the people of a society will significantly contribute to fundamental social change.

To understand the view just put forward, it is necessary to rethink the concept of power that so far has been popularly contemplated without adequate consideration of the worldviews all human beings have. Social sciences generally treat an individual as an actor who plays roles according to the institutional arrangements of the society. Besides being a rational actor, however, an individual is also a whole human. The symbolic dimension of political life is, thus, as significant as the conscious, utilitarian dimension. The power that derives from this symbolic dimension can be fully understood only in a comprehensive three-dimensional framework of analysis in which nomos, cosmos, and chaos are in constant, complex, and creative interaction with one another.

ACKNOWLEDGMENTS

THIS BOOK is not solely my product. Five extraordinary mentors helped shape my originally amorphous idea. Emiko Ohnuki-Tierney of anthropology gave me the first intellectual shock. As a result, I now look at and interpret things from a drastically different point of view. John W. Dower is more than a history teacher. Besides his distinctively deep understanding of Japanese history and society in general, I will always admire his life-style, philosophy, and academic discipline. As a political scientist, I pay my highest respect to Richard M. Merelman and Murray Edelman, whose enormous intellect and broad receptivity are responsible for developing my interdisciplinary perspective. Their constructive as well as penetrating criticisms of my manuscript encouraged me to go back to primary principles to restructure the theoretical basis. Susan J. Pharr provided me with generous intellectual and personal support, and my sincere appreciation cannot be too much.

Many of my case studies were made possible by Japanese Diet member Watanuki Tamisuke's generous acceptance of me as an observer-intern at his office and election campaign headquarters. His seven secretaries were always extremely kind and cooperative, and we enjoyed each other's company greatly. During my research in Japan, many people in academic circles, the bureaucracy, and the media provided me with invaluable help. Professor Etō Shinkichi, now president of Asia University in Tokyo, deserves my greatest appreciation.

The most stimulating experiences, however, were with the many ordinary people with whom I shared precious moments in various places and occasions during my seven-month stay in Japan. Every day I encountered something that shook the stereotypes and academic bigotry in my mind. I was constantly thrown into confusion. And yet, I found it a refreshing challenge to be in that state of creative as well as destructive cognitive anomie. It allowed me to try many disparate points of view that were far beyond my scope before.

During the final stages, I had numerous invaluable comments and suggestions from those whom I respect both intellectually and personally. They included Robert Dekle, Shigeko Fukai, Haruhiro Fukui, Ellis Krauss, Terry E. MacDougall, John McVey, T. J. Pempel and David Titus.

The Reischauer Institute of Harvard University, where I have been a research associate, was extraordinarily supportive and provided me with a wonderfully stimulating atmosphere. I thank Director Harold Bolitho and all the faculty members from the bottom of my heart. I also would like to express my heartfelt thanks to Susan Scott, Nancy Deptula, Ella Rutledge, Anne Denna, Robin Furst, Laurie Spillane, and Kuniko Yamada. My three years at the institute with them were indeed some of the best years of my life. Their friendship has been the indispensable backbone of my professional and private life.

POLITICAL LIFE IN JAPAN

Chapter One

INTRODUCTION: SYMBOLIC DIMENSION
OF POLITICAL LIFE

IN RECENT YEARS, serious academic attention has been paid to cultural particularities that previously were often regarded as irrelevant and, thus, generally were ignored by the social sciences. It has been shown abundantly by Foucault (1970, 1979a, 1980), Davis (1975), Ginzburg (1982, 1984), Guha and Spivak (1988), Scott (1989), and others that the culturally and historically situated micro-level studies are important. The activities and behavior of ordinary people in a given culture in a given historical period that are considered to be simply insignificant and apolitical are, in fact, impregnated with meaning and reflect physical conditions being experienced by those people.

The changes in these meanings and the physical environment affect the daily lives of people at a glacial pace and often go unnoticed but have the potential to create a condition conducive to drastic reorganization of a political system. It is, more importantly, at the moment of intrusion of symbolic domain into ordinary people's lifeworlds when these seemingly minor, usually invisible changes in meanings and environment may become visible, reinforced, or accelerated, or add a new direction. That is, ordinary people's symbolic experiences, that is manifestation of marginality, in their daily lives would, cumulatively, not only exert vast energy to bring the fluidity necessary for society to transform society but also would reflect the direction and nature of the changes in the making.

The value of studying people's daily particularities should then be clear, which would certainly enable us to understand minute living conditions of the people of a given culture. The supreme significance, however, is that we would be able to grasp fundamental changes in a social system and their dynamism in the whole context. That is, these minute changes in meaning and physical conditions manifested at the moment of symbolic intrusion always reflect changes in relations between ordinary people and the authorities, order, or the outside world. No matter how minor and trivial they may appear, these changes reveal the changes in the entire network of social relations.

The Concepts of Power and Change

Although power is one of the major concerns of political science studies, the very concept of power is scarcely agreed upon. A series of different approaches to the study of power have emerged[1] and most of them fall into one of three groupings, depending on whether the authors see (1) power as will, (2) power as derived from structure, or (3) power as derived from worldview. Behaviorists basically see "power as will" on the assumption that an individual's consciousness is free from structural constraints; that is, individuals have an unconstrained ability to know the truth about their wants and needs. Naturally, little attention is paid to the possibility that individual consciousness, view, and value may not be totally reducible to the individual but, instead, may be coded by a collectivity in the way it determines the scope and kinds of matters that arise in which power is manifested.

In the meantime, the "power as derived from structure" grouping consists most notably of Marxist and, generally speaking, European scholars.[2] It is presupposed that the structure decisively influences all individuals in such a way that not only their places but also their consciousness and function in society are determined by it.[3]

The term "worldview" is clearly defined by Geertz (1973, 127) to mean the picture that people of a given culture have "of the way things in sheer actuality are, their concept of nature, of self, of society." This "power as derived from worldview" grouping is interdisciplinary and embraces scholars of symbolic anthropology, phenomenology, religion, structuralism, and, to some extent, neo-Marxism as well. Gramsci's (1971) concept of hegemony[4] and Althusser and Balivar's (1970) concept of ideology based on their structuralist reinterpretation of Marx's *Capital* are among the increasing number of recent academic endeavors that may belong to the work in this group.

As structuralism and its inevitable and monstrous product, poststructuralism, have brought about a fundamental shake-up in an entire academic profession by declaring the death of the human being as the center of the universe, any and every form of systemic dominance has drawn attention from scholars of various academic disci-

---

[1] See Clegg (1989) for one of the most recent and comprehensive studies on power.

[2] On this point, see Clegg (1979, 2–4).

[3] See Miliband (1969, 1970); Poulantzas (1969, 1973); Laclau (1975); cf. Lukes (1974, 1977).

[4] See also Williams (1960) and Femia (1975).

plines. Behind this decisive trend lies an increasing realization that an individual's very *will* cannot be purely objective or independent of a worldview that inevitably patterns and determines the scope and kind of one's wants, one's analysis of self, and the whole system within which one is located, and, therefore, that the concept of power and change must take account of deeper dimensions; these may embrace the most basic aspects of human beings as biological as well as cultural and social beings.

We must ask then how a worldview is constructed and whether it is possible for individuals to keep themselves from being reified by worldviews to the degree that they cannot question them or even be aware of them. If individuals can actively influence their own world-views, then their values, perceptions, and analyses of *reality* (including things, others, self, and the whole system) would not be those of total captives. This means, for example, that they may be able to defy or relativize given definitions of themselves, resources of value, and wants and needs and thereby make them appear to be no more than arbitrary. This seems to be an absolute precondition for any group or society that asserts itself to be free and democratic regardless of its legal, political, and social arrangements. Thus, power, freedom, and democracy—these key concerns of political science—must in the end be considered as one inseparable concept whose common roots lie in the individual's ability to resist any form of reifying force.

Such a conviction is shared increasingly widely by recent interdisciplinary works. For example, Ginzburg's (1982, 1984) studies represent a new school of history whose main focus is on ordinary people's ordinary lives, collective beliefs, and mentality, and the changes occurring through various daily encounters and interactions with authorities and with people other than themselves. Clegg[5] has been trying to synthesize action and structure, and meaning and power, based upon premises of structural linguistics, mainly those of Noam Chomsky. In the meantime, Foucault's concept of power as the operation of *assujettissement*—a mechanism that transforms an individual into a subject in submission—in ubiquity and anonymity suggests that the core of power is constituted by a technology of transformation or modification of individuals' worldviews, including their perceptions of themselves, so that their wills, value systems, actions, and behavior are structured in a certain way.[6]

[5] Clegg (1975, 1976, 1977, 1979); Clegg and Dunkerley (1980).

[6] For Foucault's works most relevant to this discussion, see Foucault 1973, 1977, 1978, 1979a, 1979b, 1980, 1981, 1983). He focuses on forms of subjection and the inflections and utilization of localized systems in the operation of power. He sees power as working ubiquitously through various forms of *dispositif* (apparatus or device). A

Human beings by necessity have worldviews at any point of their lives. Without worldviews, they would be drawn into chaos. Ironically, however, for individuals to live with worldviews their *Selves* as subjects are structured in a certain way; that is, what each wants, how each thinks, and how each acts can never be left to individual genuinely free decisions. These behaviors are all bounded by individual worldviews. Worldviews, it must be emphasized, are not something that a certain individual, group, or class can simply create and impose upon others to exert control. A worldview is not subject to intentional manipulation by human beings. No human beings can be outside it. What they can do at best, if they find themselves in an advantageous position in a given society, is merely to reinforce the existing sociocultural system that rests upon, and is structured by, a particular worldview at the time.

Discussion so far leads to the conclusion that there are no genuinely free human beings whose thoughts, perceptions, and values are unbounded. This conviction shared by various disciplines in the recent past helped poststructuralism erupt. Poststructuralist works, including most notably, Derrida (1981) and Deleuze and Guattari (1977), draw attention worldwide. Poststructuralism actually should not be called an "-ism" because it is by no means a systematic body of thoughts. On the contrary, its sole aim is to *deconstruct*; it neither criticizes nor negates any particular value, principle, or ideology of the past or present. Nor does it try to replace any values, principles, or ideologies with new ones. The poststructuralists' argument derives from their realization that throughout history ideologies or principles (e.g., Western belief in the existence of one universal truth from the time of Plato and Aristotle to those of Descartes, Kant, and modern positivists), regardless of their contents, are inevitably established and constructed as a thought system, which, in turn, unavoidably structures individuals' worldviews and prescribes their wills as well as actions. Such power is well recognized and explored by Clegg, Foucault, and others, including, most notably, Marcuse.[7]

---

firmly established hierarchical power structure or strongly constituted legal system in his view, is not the basis of power. On the contrary, the power structure and legal system are regarded by Foucault as the end results of ubiquitous microphysical power operations that directly touch the souls of human beings.

[7] Marcuse (1966), in agreement with Freud, is critical of the Western rationalism that evolved from Plato to Hegel, which maintains that rational spirit is of supreme import to humans and that self-development, self-maintenance, and attainment of rational spirit should and could be attained by first conquering the power of human inner, "inferior" senses and instincts (in opposition to spirit). Marcuse recognizes the transcendental and regenerative force in human instincts and senses. They not only

When an individual reifies a certain thought system, the only way to break out of such a state is to expose the limitations of its internal logic through deconstruction.[8]

SYMBOLIC DIMENSION INDISPENSABLE FOR POWER AND CHANGE

Explicitly or implicitly, modern social sciences generally rest upon the assumption that society consists of a major, independent, conscious dimension of human activities, and a minor, negligible, unconscious dimension of activities. It is, moreover, often assumed that the latter dimension will ultimately vanish, or at least be under control, as modernization progresses. As Cohen (1976) argues, the so-called social evolution perspective is persistent among many social scientists, including Weber and Parsons. Almond and Powell (1966, 24), too, maintain that through secularization people will become increasingly rational and analytical.

The view that equates modernization with rational and practical principles overpowering symbolic principles is seriously questioned, particularly by anthropologists, and most notably by Dumont (1970), who showed in his study of the Indian caste system that the symbolic principle transcends praxis in daily social life. Ohnuki-Tierney (1984, 225), who studied hygienic practices in modern urban Japanese society, also became convinced that a view that holds that the practical principle would dominate the center of culture as modernization advances reflects the Western belief that the practical principle is an independent and objective entity. Sahlins (1976, 211) came to view even economy in the Western culture as a core of symbolic production.

Phenomenology and symbolic anthropology are particularly rich in scholars who take the symbolic, sacred dimension seriously. They question the so-called fundamental dualism of modern Western philosophy that tacitly assumes that the objective reality or truth exists

---

counter the existing principles of civilization but also transcend them so that they can be displaced by fundamentally different ones.

[8] The poststructuralist approach is popularly regarded as the one that laughs at, jokes about, and plays with the seriousness of taken-for-granted principles or thought systems (a more inclusive French word, *jue*, may be substituted for an English word, play). In fact, Derrida's style is often called playlike, and poststructuralism itself is seen as a "big joke" (a comment by a participant at the 82d American Political Science Association meeting, panel, "Power and Poststructuralism," August 29, 1986, Washington, D.C.); for Derrida's work and deconstruction in general, see Derrida (1981); Krupnic (1983); Leitch (1983); Takeda and Nagasawa (1984); also see Ryan (1983) for his effort to apply deconstruction to social and political analysis.

first and a human being's subjective cognition may or may not fully grasp it. In other words, subjective cognition and the existence of an object and truth have been thought to be two separate things.[9] Equally, scholars reject the popular notion that a life-world constitutes only one reality wherein an individual's experiences take place through unbroken and qualitatively undifferentiated time and space.

In Husserlian phenomenology, a subject's pure consciousness is considered to be the center where countless images of objects and ideas appear and disappear. Among these images and ideas, pure consciousness selects those that would, in turn, constitute the subjects' worlds as well as their consciousness as a part of that world.[10] Schutz (1970), who carried on the Husserlian tradition in sociology, recognizes multiple realities in ordinary daily life. People experience different realities, according to him, by casually paying qualitatively disparate attention to life.

Berger and Luckmann (1966) and Berger (1969) advanced the phenomenological approach. Symbolic universe or cosmos refers to a transcendental body of meanings constructed through individual externalization of subjective experiences; these are objectivized in collectivity then internalized by the individual. Through this dialectic process, a subjective (individual) as well as an objective (collective) world are established and exert legitimizing power for the ordinary life-world, or nomos. Nomos, however, has only an imperfect power to maintain order. Not only is perfect socialization of an individual impossible but qualitatively equal socialization of all groups of society is also unattainable. Anomie or chaos at the margin is, therefore, inevitable. The existence of cosmos, or a symbolic universe, is thus crucial to protect nomos, or the ordinary life-world, from intrusive chaos. We see here a picture of a three-dimensional world. Each dimension is organically interrelated with the others so that it is now possible to think dynamically about changes that take place not just in the nomos dimension but across all three dimensions.

The imperfect nature of socialization, in a phenomenological sense, would, theoretically, allow the condition in which change of

[9] Descartes contemplated that subjective cognition can grasp perfectly externally existing objective reality. Kant, too, believed in the existence of objective truth, which itself cannot be known to humans, but subjective cognition, a common ability of human beings, would allow an object to appear the same way so that objectivity is attainable, if limited. Hegel conceived a dialectic relationship between subjective cognition and an external object so that an object appears in different ways as the subject interacts with it. Furthermore, Hegel assumed that dialectic interactions between a subject and an object would help subjective cognition ultimately arrive at objective truth.

[10] For Western philosophical tradition and Husserlian phenomenology, see Ishii (1984); Natanson (1962a, 1962b), and Husserl (1967).

the dominant symbolic universe comes from within. Nonetheless, because the socialization process is likely to be accompanied by alienation and reification,[11] as Berger and Luckmann (1966) recognize, it should be enormously difficult to expect transformation from within to take place. Berger's phenomenology then offers four theoretically possible sources for neutralization of the reified state: a total collapse of social structure, that is, nomos; contact with a foreign culture and the cultural shock that results; the marginal phenomenon of social marginality (Berger and Pullberg 1965, 209–10; Berger and Luckmann 1966, 91–92); and an individual's or a collectivity's experience of *ekstasis*. The last refers to ecstasy in the actual sense of stepping out of an ordinary life-world (Berger 1963, 136), for example, when dreaming or critically ill (for an individual) or in a natural disaster or war (for a collectivity).

We note that except for a marginal phenomenon, all other potential sources are either accidental or externally oriented. It is thus obvious that neither intention nor object setting is involved in the neutralization of reification. Some may argue that phenomenology generally, including even Sartre's, which was held to be complementary with Marxism, holds that an individual's consciousness is not only free from structural constraints but also has a natural inclination to transcend the present state of being by continuously constructing the world of meaning. This concept may well lead them to think that an individual can make genuinely free, unconstrained decisions, and, hence, reification is not an ominous problem.

If the symbolic dimension is taken into account, however, the qualitative difference between a mere aggregation of individuals and a collectivity should be immediately recognized. That is, as Durkheim (1965) argues, a collectivity acquires its own irreducible, and either repressive or legitimizing, quality, which is then imposed upon all individual subjectivities that constitute it. Cosmos represents a sacred order, which contrasts that of nomos, that has been and is being institutionalized through the experiences of a people. In relation to nomos structure, cosmos thus stands as "another structure." In the same vein, chaos is defined as *nonstructure*. The point is that cosmos might consist of principles that are contradictory and in-

---

[11] Alienation is a "process by which the unity of producing and the products is broken" so that the "product now appears to the producer as an alien facticity and power standing in itself and over against him, no longer recognizable as a product." One example of alienated consciousness is found in "the religious interpretations of the human world as merely a reflection of a divine world." And, reification refers to "the moment in the process of alienation in which the characteristics of thing-hood becomes the standard of objective reality" (Berger and Pullberg 1965, 200).

compatible with those of nomos. The phenomenological approach tends to pay insufficient attention to this aspect. Consequently, a crucial problem is left unsolved: that is, a focal point that enables transformation of subjective realities into the qualitatively disparate and irreducible collectivity's reality is missing. One possible bridge between subjective and objective realities is symbolism, as abundantly demonstrated in V. Turner's studies (1974, 1977).

This comparison leads to symbolic anthropology, which may provide a clue about how the reification process can be neutralized by means other than accidental or external factors, and to which the study of marginal quality—the only nonexternal, nonaccidental source listed by Berger, Berger and Luckman, and Berger and Pullberg—chiefly belongs. V. Turner's (1974, 1977) notions of *communitas* and *structure* have been well established in social sciences. He developed Van Gennep's (1960) three-phase ritual process of separation→margin (or limen)→reaggregation to holistically conceptualize a society (or societas, as he calls it) as consisting of two dialectically interrelated structures—a matrix of roles and statuses, where ordinary, profane preoccupations are dominant, and communitas, where an individual transcends the state of the profane, separate being to reach the higher state of being part of a collectivity of equal whole-humans. V. Turner (1977, 132, 138) uses the term *existential*, which shares the same etymological origin with *ecstasy*, to describe this state in which an individual stands outside of the social structure, here, existence means nothing but being in ecstasy.[12]

It is at the middle phase, that is, the liminal or marginal phase, when communitas overpowers structure. It is the symbolic phase at which structural *invalidation* (V. Turner 1968,576) occurs. Because the distinctive arrangements of positions in the preritual structure are symbolically "dead," people gain a chance to "become aware of all positions and arrangements" (p. 577). As a consequence, and through the use of "cultural inventory" (p. 577) any rearrangement becomes possible.

V. Turner advanced Van Gennep's formulation significantly so that

[12] Because humans can by no means maintain their lives in a world of fragmented roles and statuses, and because they need to regain the state of being whole-humans occasionally, their entrance into egalitarian, nonutilitarian, spontaneous, and aesthetic communitas is an absolute necessity for their very existence. The impulse toward communitas is not conceived by V. Turner (1977, 128) in terms of psychology, or social psychology, or functionalism. He thinks it is the product of unique human faculties that develop through experiences in social life; although it is certainly true, as psychological or functionalistic explanations (e.g., that of Gluckman [1954, 1962]) hold, that through communitas, human instinctive energy reaches an extraordinarily high level and is discharged.

communitas, or the liminal phase, can be thought of in a broader context. That is, communitas not only appears in the midphase, or the ritual process, but also tends to be embodied by marginal beings and accompanies liminal states, which are found in the interstices of social structure, on its margin, or on its bottom layer. To mention a few examples here, marginal beings include conquered indigenous people, court jesters, Gypsies, outcastes, prostitutes, hippies, and minor religious groups, and so on whereas liminal states may accompany millenarian movements, matrilineal lineages in societies centered on patrilineal lineages, wars, festivals, plays, and travels.

Those beings regarded as marginal, inferior, or misfit in terms of social structure are, nevertheless, an indispensable, regenerative source for the society. They can be dangerous intruders and destroyers of social structure but, at the same time, can be reactivators and regenerators of it. As V. Turner (1977, 128) puts it, "Communitas breaks in through the interstices of structure, in liminality; at the edges of structure, in marginality; and from beneath structure, in inferiority." In a word, symbolic communitas, which is characteristically antistructure, manifests a crucial dimension of human relations and is ready to appear whenever a void or fragility in structure is found.

Deformative/Transformative Qualities of Liminality

The foregoing establishes a general idea of what comprises the power of a human being. It must work in such a way that most taken-for-granted, comprehensive ideas, values, and principles are shaken, relativized, invalidated, and disintegrated to keep an individual from being reified. If individuals are able to question their own subjectivity and the perceptions of others and of the entire system of which they are a part, they can resist encroachment by often unnoticed, indiscriminate, and ubiquitous operations of power at the deepest level of human life. And this ability is called *reflexivity*.[13] Reflexivity, as Babcock (1980, 2) puts it, is "the capacity of language and of thought— of any system of signification—to turn or bend back upon itself, to become an object itself, and to refer to itself." Individuals who can equip themselves with active reflexivity may be able to defy the prescribed scope and type of behavior and thought and thereby resist control by any form of authority (e.g., ideology, language, religion,

[13] On reflexivity, see also Rappaport (1980); Myerhoff and Ruby (1982).

law, and sciences) that has developed its *raison d'être* on the basis of the existing system.

As both Babcock (1980, 2–6) and V. Turner (1974, 255) point out, liminality provides the occasions for reflexivity when, through the reorganization of experience, "the free recombination of the factors of culture into any and every possible pattern" (V. Turner 1974, 255) takes place. This reorganization, in turn, enables us "to know ourselves and our world, to know how we know, to reflect on our own interpretive processes" (Babcock 1980, 6). Terrence Turner's (1977) analysis of the liminal phase of Van Gennep's rites of passage dissects it even more compellingly. In his efforts to articulate the logic of transformation, he argues that "the phenomena of the liminal phase constitute, in structural terms, a different (and higher) level of the same system of relations as that represented by the secular order of social relations" (T. Turner 1977, 54). More concretely, he means that when, for instance, a boy becomes a man through certain rites of passage, the transition from boy to man involves the merger and inversion of two exclusive sets of role categories of boy and man so that the actor can relate two sets of roles, "not as it were within the same state of the matrix of role relations, but as components of two different states of the same matrix related by transformation" (T. Turner 1977, 55).

T. Turner's analysis of the logic and mechanisms of transformation permits us to clarify our understanding of the meaning and nature of liminality. Kapferer (1979), for instance, rests upon T. Turner's logic that a transformation of context might take place when ambiguities and inconsistencies appear in the organization of action and meaning. In addition, he holds that the merger of different, often mutually contradictory, contexts will inevitably bring about inconsistencies and ambiguities; these, in turn, would urge reestablishment of consistency. This very process, he maintains, constitutes a transformation of context through the rearrangement or reordering of organization of the component elements of one context at a higher level and thereby gives rise to a different context of action and meaning.

That marginal beings and liminal states necessarily and characteristically embody ambiguity and contradiction is a thesis fully supported by a number of scholars besides V. Turner.[14] Because of their domain of existence between either nomos and cosmos or nomos and chaos, any marginal being and liminal state must be inherently em-

---

[14] See also Leach (1961a, 1961b, 1964, 1967, 1976); Lévi-Strauss (1963); Douglas (1966, 1970); Babcock-Abrahams (1975); Yamaguchi (1975); and Ohnuki-Tierney (1984, chap. 2).

bodying mutually incompatible sets of values, views, and principles—or a total lack of them—of two or more contrasting domains. Even the mere presence of marginal beings or liminal states, therefore, would cause inconsistencies and ambiguities to nomos.

Handelman and Kapferer (1980)[15] have already presented serious studies that treated marginal beings and liminal states as media for contextual transformation. They suggest two types of symbolic figures: an initiator of contextual transformation and a potential agent of transformation. One type may be adequately called a *deformer* instead of transformer, even though by deforming the context this type allows the possibility of transformation. The marginal beings and liminal states dealt with throughout this book belong to this type. By bringing in inconsistencies, contradictions, and ambiguities, marginal beings and liminal states deform—or at least shake—the context. Transformation may or may not occur as a consequence. Chaos could follow. Still, the significance of marginal beings and liminal states as deformers is that they ceaselessly shake the whole context. This means that they relativize everything, and they reveal the arbitrariness of any of the taken-for-granted things, principles and people. In so doing, marginal beings and liminal states would offer ordinary people opportunities to reexamine and comment on existing arrangements, that is, to help people keep themselves from being reified.

The other types of symbolic figures noted by Handelman and Kapferer (1980) resemble Weber's charisma. Each has its own consistent worldview; each will try to transform the exiting context into one that fits its own worldview. They would destroy the old context only to impose another. Ordinary people, in this case, are, at best, passive participants in the transformation but neither initiators of nor a central force for it. This kind of transformative change, moreover, will likely take place as an extraordinary social event. Ordinary people's daily behavior and activities are not an essential component of such events.

In contrast, the deformation marginal beings and liminal states constantly involve ordinary people's daily behavior and activities directly. The deformers operate at the micro level. The changes, if not always transformative, will arise from interstices, marginal edges, and bottom levels and are ubiquitous, even while often unrecognized. Unlike transformative changes led by charisma, no alternative worldview will be imposed. Whatever the consequences may be, the deformative changes take shape from what ordinary people are do-

---

[15] See also Kapferer (1979).

ing in their daily lives. Marginal beings and liminal states, thus, provide ordinary people with conditions in which they unintentionally participate in the process of social change as an active central force. No one, however, can predict where the changes will lead. Neither marginal beings nor liminal states have anything to do with the contents of such changes nor do they direct their courses.

In any event, few scholars see predominant, regenerative force in liminality. Interpretations range from those of sociologists like Erikson (1966, 19), who regard marginal beings as a "bit of debris spun out by faulty social machinery," to more sympathetic Durkheim (1964), who considers them to be an inevitable part of social organization, and to Douglas (1968, 1970), who as, Babcock-Abrahams (1975, 155) points out, in contrast to her previous work (Douglas 1966) shows proclivity for treating them like subsidiaries. A more recent generation of scholars, such as Moore and Myerhoff (1975), who are under the influence of V. Turner, generally hold that at best what marginal beings and liminal states could do is to strengthen or consolidate the dominant social structure. A few, however, recognize much more active and positive aspects of liminality. Yamaguchi (1969, 1975, 1977a, 1977b) consistently maintains that liminality can be a crucial activator of the structure. So do Babcock-Abrahams (1975), Kapferer (1979), and Handelman and Kapferer (1980), who draw our attention to a more creative, transformative aspect of marginal beings and liminal states.

In the study presented here, I will attempt to construct a generalized concept of liminality—its nature, characteristics, and the way it affects and interacts with the dominant structure. Although T. Turner and Kapferer help us understand the logic of change that is invoked by marginal beings or in liminal states, their cases are largely confined to small community rituals, as are many anthropological studies. Therefore, liminality and transformation or deformation tend to be thought of within the framework of community rituals, if not necessarily those of a religious kind. Modern anthropological studies consist of intensive participatory field research. This method is considered crucial, especially since Malinowski, for understanding a native culture. Nonetheless, it may almost by necessity prevent scholars from dealing with broader social dynamics. Social transformation is not likely to be their prime interest.[16]

In the meantime, the main interest in this study lies in dynamic, progressive, and irreversible social change—that is, the logic and

---

[16] It should be noted here that in recent years a new movement has occurred in anthropology toward a study of modern societies.

mechanism of social transformation,—and not in change that involves merely cyclical alternation of the state of being. As has been discussed so far, this kind of fundamental change must involve neutralization of the force of reification. Neutralization can be attained by keeping reflexivity active, and reflexivity operates chiefly in the symbolic and unconscious dimension. Anthropology tells how reflexivity can be kept active. The belief that inconsistencies, ambiguities, and contradictions brought about by marginal beings and liminal states would rouse ordinary people's reflexivity so that a new consistency can be established under a new organizational principle that accommodates both old and new elements invokes confidence. A reified state thus cannot be rigidified or even simply maintained as long as marginal beings and liminal states keep intruding spatially and temporally into the nomos structures and thereby rouse people's sense of need to reorder the existing institutional arrangements under a new principle.

Manifestation of Liminality in the Life-World of Ordinary People

How such intrusion into and overpowering of the existing order by marginal beings and liminal states can take place needs to be clarified. V. Turner, based on his abundant field studies, believes that liminality overpowers structures with a flow of symbols. Leach (1961b) discerns the logic of Durkheim's analysis of religious rites (i.e., collective boiling in the sacred) and divides it into three qualitatively disparate temporal phases: entering the sacred, liminality, and departing from the sacred. This process can be invoked by contrasting a category of social structure with another whose organizational principle is the inverse of that of the former, according to Leach.

Leach's logical explanation is congruent with the theses of T. Turner and Kapferer, as seen; the presence of contradiction will be accompanied by the operation at a higher level (i.e., cosmos rather than nomos). This understanding also enables us to consider the possibility that the logic of contradiction→liminality→deformation/transformation may be extended so that it can acquire a broader applicability. Leach's discerning analysis suggests that even a sacred religious ritual operates with a logic that can be extended to any ordinary secular context as well. To reiterate, the process of contradiction→liminality→deformation/transformation necessarily involves activation of reflexivity and neutralization of a reified state, and this process constitutes the core of power of ordinary people. Marginal beings and liminal states that have the potential to bring about this process, therefore, are absolutely indispensable when we conceive of such power.

By now the characteristics of marginal beings and liminal states should be obvious. We can enumerate them based on countless studies of liminality: carrying multiple identities or none; dualism of being, for instance, creative as well as destructive; and defiance of any kind toward existing authority or order. In concrete form, liminality tends to manifest in tricksters,[17] fools,[18] strangers,[19] executioners,[20] marginal man,[21] punks and hipsters,[22] the beat generation,[23] rappers,[24] black radicals,[25] social bandits,[26] artists, especially, such as symbolists and surrealists,[27] university students of Europe in the Middle Ages,[28] itinerant healers/priests, fortune-tellers, entertainers, criminals, beggars, the physically/mentally handicapped (e.g., the blind, stutterers, and the deaf), outcastes,[29] and intellectuals.[30]

Because of their places in interstices, at the margin, or bottom of the nomos structure, they have a greater potential and liability to embody liminal qualities and to experience liminality. Ordinary people have the same potential and liability, if to a lesser degree. The potential and liability of ordinary people would be invoked by the intrusions of marginal beings and liminal states into their life-worlds. Ordinary people thereby would experience moments when they embodied liminal qualities or entered liminal phases.

Liminality may appear in the form of an extraordinary state such as millenarian or messianic movements during periods of social ca-

---

[17] Wescott (1962); Lévi-Strauss (1963); V. Turner (1968, 580–581); Cox (1969); Radin (1969); Yamaguchi (1974, 1977a); Babcock-Abrahams (1975); cf. Beidelman (1980).

[18] Welsford (1935); Willeford (1969); Yamaguchi (1969). Refer also to Erasmus (1965) and an insightful interpretation of his thought by Huizinga (1952); another interesting study of a modern fool, skew media, is presented by Seymour-Ure (1974).

[19] Schutz (1944); Simmel (1950, 402–8); Frankenberg (1957); Ohnuki-Tierney (1984, chap. 2).

[20] Abe (1978).

[21] Stonequist (1937).

[22] Mailer (1959).

[23] Lipton (1959).

[24] Pareles (1990).

[25] Malcolm X (1966).

[26] Hobsbawm (1960).

[27] Marcuse (1969, 1972, 1978).

[28] Cleugh (1963, 75–82).

[29] Yokoi (1975, 316–27); Abe (1981); Ohnuki-Tierney (1984, chap. 2).

[30] Mannheim (1936, 153–64); Berger and Luckmann (1966, 10, 125–28) Inoue et al. (1977, 179–82).

tastrophe,[31] war,[32] festival or carnival,[33] journey and pilgrimage,[34] and various kinds of religious rituals. Nonetheless, ordinary people's experiences in entering liminal states are by no means confined to extraordinary occasions. In ubiquitous, trivial human activities and behavior, moments of manifestation of the liminal are abundant in any cultural context: joking and laughter,[35] comic myths,[36] riddles,[37] daydreams and fantasies,[38] play,[39] and all those behaviors and activities that invoke ecstatic experiences ranging from gift giving (potluch in the extreme), to art, sex (especially that for unreproductive purposes), drinking/dining together, dancing, especially with intense physical movements, to explosive orgies as studied and interpreted so fascinatingly in imaginative works.[40]

The particular interest in this book is neither to study the special kinds of people or things that are situated at the margin, in the interstices, or on the bottom of the nomos structure nor to deal with major extraordinary affairs like war and natural disaster. It is the trivial, seemingly insignificant daily particularities of ordinary people—that is, ordinary people's experiences of symbolic intrusions into their daily life-worlds—that will interest us most.

THE STRUCTURE OF A WORLDVIEW

It is now appropriate to explain with logical clarity how these marginal beings and liminal states commonly could have effects that help reactivate the reflexivity of ordinary people. The task requires combining insights from structuralism, poststructuralism, symbolic anthropology, phenomenology, structural linguistics, and semiotics and begins with a reconceptualization of the fundamental structure of a worldview.

[31] Shepperson and Price (1958); Cohn (1961, 1970); Newfield (1966); Nishigaki (1977).

[32] Caillois (1959, 163–80).

[33] Caillois (1959); Hayakawa (1966); McGlashan (1967); Yamaguchi (1969); Bakhtin (1984).

[34] Karve (1962); Malcolm X (1966); Jiménez (1972); V. Turner (1977).

[35] Bergson (1956), Freud (1963); Havránek (1964); Douglas (1968); Bastide (1970); Yamaguchi (1977a).

[36] Clastres (1977, 108–27).

[37] Hamnett (1967).

[38] Marcuse (1966, 140–58).

[39] Bataille (1951); Huizinga (1955); Schiller (1965); Marcuse (1966, 172–96); Geertz (1972); Yokoi et al. (1986); cf. Caillois (1959, 152–62; 1961).

[40] See Bataille (1949, 1951, 1954, 1957, 1973); Marcuse (1966, 1969, 1972, 1978); Yamaguchi (1969, 1975); V. Turner (1974, 1977); and Kurimoto (1979, 1980, 1981).

Structuralism was developed by Lévi-Strauss, who had been inspired by the theory of linguist Ferdinand de Saussure. Saussure (1966) defined two dialectically interrelated principles in language: syntagmatic relationship and associational relationship among words. The former is essentially a linear, irreversible, and connected relationship between two consecutive words. In the latter, words are related deep in the unconscious sphere, and each word pops up in daily conversation as cued by an individual's or collectivity's past memory, similarity in sound or meaning, and so forth. Syntagmatic: associational principle in language was then redefined as a metonymy: metaphor complementary opposition model to apply it to broader areas of human activities and behavior.[41]

Let us contrast a metonymic with a metaphoric relationship here by using some examples:

Metonymy		*Metaphor*	
ash......	charcoal	ash......	phoenix
grapes...	wine	grapes...	fox
rose.....	thorn	rose.....	war
sea......	water	sea......	crowd
time.....	clock	time.....	arrow
veil.....	bride	veil.....	fog

In a metonymic relationship, only interconnected words can be put together in a hierarchical or causal relationship. In contrast, in a metaphor, any two or more words can be put together horizontally in a reversible, arbitrary relationship. Any human behavior and activity can be categorized into either of these complementary opposites, metonymy-metaphor. For example, surrealist poems and paintings, gossiping, barbecuing, gambling, and daydreaming, as well as telegraphs, advertisements, and newspapers, as imaginatively reinterpreted by McLuhan (1964), are all metaphors. However, legal documents, detective stories, trade negotiations, driving a car, keeping a household account, and having power lunches fall into the metonymy group. Lévi-Strauss (1966) categorized scientific human activities as metonymic because they try to analyze relationships among objects in terms of cause and effect. In contrast, artistic activities, in general, may be regarded as metaphoric because they select objects in the world of imagination according to their associational closeness.

Some may be tempted to think that metonymy and metaphor correspond to V. Turner's structure and communitas, respectively. Or,

---

[41] See Jakobson (1963, 1971).

to use more ordinary terms, this pair may match the praxis:symbolic complementary opposition.

Metonymy = Structure = Praxis

Metaphor = Communitas = Symbolic

As repeatedly argued so far, unlike those popular theories and perspectives of the social sciences, which tend to confine their attention to human behavior and activities within the structure, we see communitas or the symbolic dimension as no less significant and substantial than the structure. If we think in terms of the metonymy-metaphor complementary opposition, for the sake of convenience, it is easy to see that there should not and cannot be an inferior-superior relationship between these two dimensions.

Lévi-Strauss (1966) and his best critic, Leach (1976), as Beck (1978) suggests, disagree on the status of metonymy and metaphor. Lévi-Strauss believes that although metaphor is accompanied by holistic, abstract thought, metonymy involves concrete reasoning and that metaphor is at a higher level and metonymy is at a lower level. That is, although all human minds use concrete, physical, linear thinking to a degree, a savage mind uses it more often than a modern scientific mind does. Leach, however, contemplates it the other way around. In his belief, the basic human understanding of the external world involves an arbitrary, metaphoric logic, namely, an application of sensory inputs to a set of binary categories. Metonymic logic, according to him, then, is structured in the subsequent process of reasoning, which ultimately leads to abstract ideas. From their arguments, it should be apparent that the two dimensions are in a mutually indispensable and complementary relationship. Moreover, Ohnuki-Tierney's (1990) insight suggests that metaphor and metonymy are interpenetrable with each other and their nature is contextually determined.

Neither focusing on only one dimension nor arguing about the superiority or inferiority of either, therefore, is adequate or worthwhile. Ohnuki-Tierney's argument also suggests the important point that there should be no activities, people, things, or principles that have absolutely fixed value and meaning regardless of context. To put it more concretely, we should not take, for example, President George Bush as the fixed occupant of the center. Neither should we define colored foreign laborers in Japan as marginals regardless of the context. Their meaning, category, and relationships with others are constantly shifting in the process of contextual changes.

In any event, given a parallel between structure = praxis = metonymy and communitas = symbolic = metaphor, a constructive way to deal with social dynamics holistically is to help build a comprehensive model of worldview. To this end, Berger's (1969) conceptualization of a three-dimensional symbolic universe and Ueno's (1977) refinement of it are extremely useful. It enables us to explain logically how changes take place.

Figure 1.1 is a further modified conceptualization of worldview. Each domain is always defined in relation to the other two. Nomos needs cosmos's sacred order to maintain legitimacy and meaningfulness to life within. This need of cosmos by nomos derives from the latter's vulnerability to the tendency to fall into chaos. The existence of chaos is crucial to cosmos, whose need to strengthen and consolidate itself can be met by exposure to an external threat, that is, an invasion by chaos. Nomos, cosmos, and chaos are thus in an intricately complementary relationship. The key to this new model is its incorporation of a marginal/liminal domain between cosmos and nomos and between chaos and nomos. The existence of the liminal domain and the inherent function of cosmos, nomos, and chaos as a mediator allow them to be in dynamic and organic interactions with one another. In short, it is a marginal/liminal domain that gives dynamism to the three dimensions of nomos, cosmos, and chaos and thereby makes three-dimensional change, that is, transformation, possible.

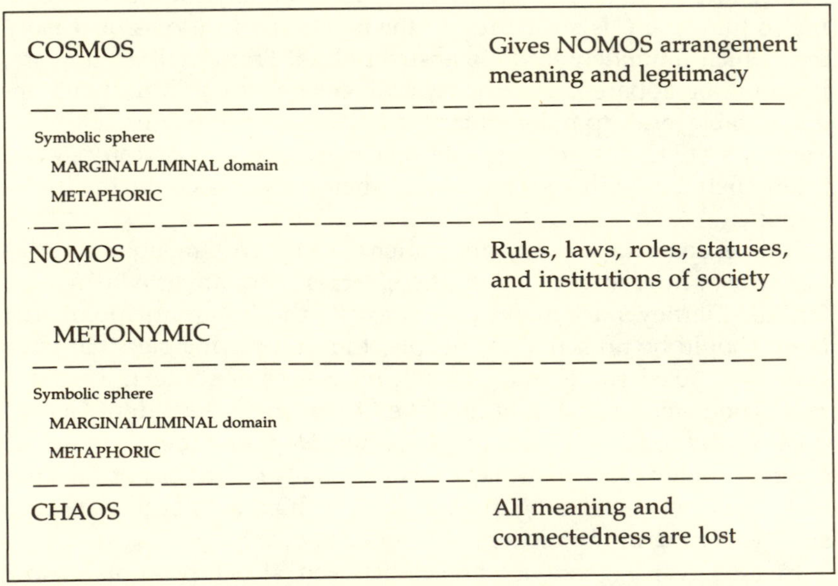

COSMOS	Gives NOMOS arrangement meaning and legitimacy
— — — — — — — — — — — — —	— — — — — — — — —
Symbolic sphere MARGINAL/LIMINAL domain METAPHORIC	
— — — — — — — — — — — — — — —	— — — — — — —
NOMOS	Rules, laws, roles, statuses, and institutions of society
METONYMIC	
— — — — — — — — — — — — —	— — — — — — — —
Symbolic sphere MARGINAL/LIMINAL domain METAPHORIC	
— — — — — — — — — — — — — —	— — — — — — —
CHAOS	All meaning and connectedness are lost

Figure 1.1. Three-dimensional Worldview

For easier comprehension, cosmos may be represented by God/ heavenly law; nomos, by human/this-worldly order; and chaos, by wild animal/no order. The liminal and metaphoric domain is resided in by all the marginal beings and liminal states (V. Turner's "be-twixt"), listed in the preceding section. It should be reiterated here with special emphasis that marginal beings and liminal states are nei-ther fixed nor exclusive to certain categories of people or particular states of being. Ordinary people in their daily lives have moments in which they themselves become marginal beings or enter liminal states. Ordinary people, too, have the potential and liability to em-body liminality.

To persons in nomos, their worlds—to follow Leach (1976), *A*—face another world, *not-A*, which can be either cosmos, whose prin-ciple for ordering its component elements contrasts with that of their ordinary life-worlds, nomos, or chaos, where no ordering principle is found. For example, in nomos, all creatures, including human be-ings, are mortal. In another world, in cosmos or heaven, however, that principle is inverted, and none are mortal, or even aged. It is a world that defies both temporal and spatial constraints. Or, to take a more familiar example, whether it is Christianity, Buddhism, Shin-toism, or Islam, the religious definition (cosmos) of people and val-ues (e.g., what constitutes sin, beauty, and so forth), is often not quite compatible with those of ordinary people's life-worlds (nomos). A Japanese politician who managed to get acquitted of a corruption charge would unlikely feel himself clean and free. Cosmos of his worldview would remain unsettled after this disturbance and, as Geertz (1973, 126) states, would make him feel "the powerfully co-ercive 'ought' " to be properly purified of his sin according to the cosmos law, in this case, by winning back in the next election, one of the modern versions of the Shintoist purification ritual.

The point here is that nomos stands in contradiction to both cos-mos and chaos, although in a peculiarly disparate way to each. Be-cause of that stand, metaphoric marginal beings and liminal states inevitably embody contradiction; that is, without fail they carry char-acteristics of both *A* and *not-A* worlds at the same time. Their pres-ence, which in itself results in an infusion of *not-A* elements into an *A* world, is, therefore, naturally destructive and threatening to *A*. Yet it can be regenerative as well because the intrusions of inconsistency will inevitably call for reestablishment of consistency under a new organizational principle.

It should be clear here that cosmos, nomos, and chaos are in an organic, tripartite relationship involving all three at the same time by necessity owing to the mediation of the marginal/liminal domain. In other words, this cosmos-nomos-chaos model should not be regarded as a synthesis of pairs of complementary oppositions—for example, cosmos-nomos plus chaos-nomos. Scholars ranging from Durkheim, Eliade and Lévi-Strauss, to Douglas, who conceive of two-dimensional worlds, although each in a uniquely disparate way, tend to see changes as cyclical alternations. Naturally, symbolic renewal of cosmos, for instance, is, in fact, reinforcement of the structure of the system rather than transformation of it. It is the static nature of their analysis and the systemic stability it implies that are being criticized by the poststructuralists.

The three-dimensional model presented here, in the meantime, is designed to deal with real social dynamics, that is, progressive and irreversible changes involving all three dimensions through the mediation of a marginal/liminal domain that lies on the fringe and in the interstices of nomos. As just mentioned, the three-dimensional, progressive, and irreversible changes are constantly made available because the intrusions of the liminal indiscriminately and ubiquitously call structure into question.

All marginal beings and liminal states commonly introduce into nomos multidimensional, discontinuous, skewed, mutually contradictory, spare, strange, and inclusive elements of reality in an unorganized, disconnected (i.e., metaphoric) fashion. Unlike metonymy—in which reason, causality, and order are already accomplished in one domain of thought—the metaphorically presented *in-the-process* reality forces people to involve themselves voluntarily, actively, and creatively in the reorganization and reconstruction of a new reality. This reorganization takes place upon the intrusions of marginal/liminal domain into nomos. The consequence is boundary blurring or boundary breaking. In other words, it inevitably involves deformation and/or a shake-up of the nomos order. It casts doubt on everything in nomos, no matter how firmly established something may appear to be in the existing value system of nomos. It is an opportunity for ordinary people to reflect and comment on themselves and the whole system within which they are located. It is, in a word, a moment for ordinary people to have their reflexivity activated and reactivated.

CASE STUDIES

In the following chapters, I will analyze several concrete cases that involve marginal beings and liminal states in various forms found mainly in contemporary Japanese political life. Attention will be paid especially to those cases in which marginal beings and liminal states, in a Japanese cultural context, are observed, ranging from an individual who happens to be situated at the sociocultural and/or political margin at a certain time in history under certain circumstances to an orgy at an election campaign headquarters, and to shedding tears and play, which serve as deformers or agents of transformation.

In chapter 2 I introduce, the Lower House Finance Committee of the Japanese Parliament (Diet) to shed fresh light on an academically neglected aspect of the relationships and daily interactions among members of the opposition and ruling Liberal Democratic party (LDP). I will suggest that a popular assumption to the effect that the legislative process consists of two or more adversarial parties, each of which competes for the attainment of its own goals, needs to be reconsidered.

Through a succession of intrusions of liminal states into their daily interactions, the opposition and LDP members steadily build a relationship that rests on their total involvement as human beings, not merely a so-called working relationship in which people, as "actors," interact with each other according to their formal roles, statuses, and other institutional arrangements. Viewing this the other way around, we can state that a series of shared liminal experiences among the opposition and LDP members contributes to the creation of a condition that allows the possibility of deformation of the existing context to arise. Boundaries among their roles, statuses, and ideological categories eventually appear ambiguous to the legislators; and party lines, laws, and rules appear arbitrary. The legislative process in the Japanese Diet, consequently, often involves a merger of two or more mutually incompatible views and policy stances rather than conflicts and compromises between clearly demarcated policies on particular issues. The main focus of the study presented here will be on what members of the Finance Committee in particular, and Diet members in general, do in their daily interactions, how a succession of intrusions of liminal states takes place in these interactions, and how that affects the committee members and the entire political system.

I devote the second section of chapter 2 to the description and analysis of occurrences at an election campaign headquarters in order to understand the meaning of an election to a candidate, local people, and the entire community. Like the case in the preceding section, here again, the key is the building of a whole-human-to-whole-human relationship, or merger, between a candidate and voters as well as among the people at large of the community. This section is intended partly to avoid giving readers an impression that what the preceding section has shown is not much different from a familiar political theory of elite accommodation—that is, coordination of horizontal relationships among the people. Marginal beings and liminal states could deform any context regardless of its content, whether horizontal (elite-elite) or vertical (elite-mass). From a practical point of view, an election campaign, especially management of a campaign headquarters, is rather wasteful and inefficient, as will be shown. Nonetheless, if viewed as an occasion during which a candidate and the local people experience oneness in an orgiastic time and space, its symbolic meaning is extremely significant. Our analysis thus focuses on the symbolic dimension of an election in contemporary Japanese political life.

In chapter 3, I examine comedians and laughter, play and shedding tears in Japanese culture, and find in them a common, fascinating nature and function unique to the liminal states. These seemingly insignificant liminal states are potential agents of far-reaching social change as much as, for example, major political leaders. I will also argue that neither our daily lives nor our history constitutes occurrences in a linear sequence or in a hierarchical order. Rather, numerous little catastrophes take place so that the flow of ordinary time of nomos is minced by bits of symbolic time and space. Consequently, an ordinary course of events is disrupted and bent in myriad ways. It is a chain of occurrences, each of which is mutually unrelated or contradictory. History at all levels, in other words, is something that is by nature incompatible with, and beyond, any intentional human endeavors.

In chapter 4, I introduce individual politicians in whom liminality is embodied at certain moments in history under certain circumstances. Ethnologists study "real" marginal figures who are most vividly represented by tricksters in indigenous cultures, legends, or mythologies. As a political scientist who is interested in the politics of dynamic contemporary society I will identify and extract liminal qualities from colorful tales of figures such as tricksters. This process will help us find out whether liminality may be embodied in ordinary people, or in this case, even in politicians, core supporters of nomos order, who are situated at the center of nomos institutions.

A politician in whom liminality is embodied does not intentionally manipulate symbols. Unlike a charismatic leader, the politician does not impose an alternative systematic worldview on people to bring about change. Rather, the politician unwittingly—as a matter of fact, by presence itself—helps expose the internal inconsistencies and limits of the existing order and helps deform it. In this way, a politician in whom liminality manifests itself under certain temporal and spatial conditions provides ordinary people with an opportunity to reactivate their reflexivity; that is, the politician forces ordinary people to reexamine and comment on themselves—who they are, how they are, how they know they are, how the existing social arrangements are, and so forth.

In the concluding chapter, the first focus will be to examine how a three-dimensional change could occur and what the significance of a liminal domain is to that change. In the latter section, we will rethink some of the most frequently used but never agreed upon terms in political science circles, in particular, and in society in general. These terms include power, social change, freedom, democracy, and individualism as a basis of democracy.

Chapter Two

POLITICAL RITUALS

THE ABSTRACT, theoretical discussions in chapter 1 would be enriched with concrete cases that show how maginal beings and liminal states actually deform the context and help people create an occasion for both activating reflexivity and experiencing whole-human-to-whole-human relationships with others. In this chapter, we will examine ubiquitous occurrences, some obvious and others extremely subtle. In the first section, we deal with the behavior and activities of the Japanese legislators in the Diet, especially those of the members of the Lower House Finance Committee. We will observe closely how the members go through a number of liminal experiences together. Although each one of these seemingly trivial ritual occasions looks too insignificant to be taken seriously, in a myriad, such symbolic experiences are as substantial as laws, regulations, and other physical, material resources. In a later section, we will devote fresh attention to an election campaign. The focus will be specifically on a Diet member's campaign headquarters in order to examine what an election means to both a candidate-politician and the people of the constituency. We will see an election as much more an occasion for ritual exchanges between people and a candidate than a somber opportunity for voters to exercise their rights.

Informal Social Activities of the Finance Committee in the Japanese Diet

I chose the politicians'—rather than ordinary people's—behavior and activities on and off the Diet floor as a focus of this study to show that even in such a place as the Diet, where behavior and activities are supposed to be more strictly regulated and roles and statuses are more clearly and rigidly defined than in most institutions in society, the inevitability and ubiquity of the occurrence of intrusions of liminal domain are obvious. This focus would also reveal that the political elite's informal, nonpolitical behavior and the activities that are commonly observed in ordinary people's daily lives have as much significant political potential as their conscious, calculated political actions do.

Careful analysis of the Japanese legislators' informal behavior and activities reveals that shared experiences of liminality and whole-human-to-whole-human relationships among them allow for the condition in which they could transcend party lines, boundaries of roles and statuses and laws. Consequently, a persistent and extraordinary merger of views and policies has been taking place between the numerically inferior, unaligned opposition and the dominant Liberal Democratic party (LDP) during the latter's thirty-five-year rule.

Several studies of the formal legislative process have been presented.[1] Yet, whether such formal rules and laws are substantially relied on or maintained primarily for formality's sake has not been sufficiently examined. A few of the most recent studies, such as those by Krauss (1982, 1984), Mochizuki (1982), Satō and Matsuzaki (1986), and Iwai (1988) pay fresh attention to the real practices, and hence see a more active role on the part of the opposition.

Nonetheless, what the members of the opposition parties and the ruling LDP actually do to bring an accord that serves the interests of both sides is not given sufficient attention. Krauss (1984, 252–53) and Satō and Matsuzaki (1986, 129–30) point out that the opposition's rejection of the discussion or boycott of the Diet sessions (*shingi kyohi*) as well as the ruling LDP's snap vote (*kyōkō saiketsu*) are often done only after both sides have reached a tacit agreement. Both sides usually decide how to resolve the expected accompanying tension before actually launching the snap vote or boycott.[2] It is then suggested that the Diet session can be seen more appropriately to be functioning as a theater where the Diet members are performing to the national audience, rather than as a place for real, substantial discussions (Satō and Matsuzaki 1986).[3]

Either way, however, these studies more or less share the assumption that what one has (i.e., resources, potential as well as actual) matters. More concretely, it is assumed that the number of the Diet seats, among other things, does count substantially in the legislative process. This basic assumption seems to agree with the popular image that because the LDP maintained an uninterrupted majority rule for thirty-five years since its formation in 1955, the opposition has been ineffective and had little relevance. Another related popular no-

---

[1] See, for example, Baerwald (1974); Kojima (1979); Iwai (1984); and Murakawa (1985).

[2] On this point, see the vivid accounts of the two veteran Diet members, Socialist, Yamamoto (1988), and LDP, Kuno (1988).

[3] In this connection, also see Tanaka (1981, chap. 3), who identifies the relationship between the LDP and the opposition as that of an actor in the title role and a supporting actor on the stage of the Diet theater.

tion holds that when the number of LDP seats is greater, the successful passage rate of government-sponsored bills will be higher,
whereas, the percentage of the revised and/or resolution-attached
bills will be lower.

In figure 2.1 we see that neither the LDP's numerical strength nor
the length of a Diet term is correlated with the successful passage of
government-sponsored bills in any meaningful way. More significantly, the success rate of government-sponsored bills and the percentage of those bills that are revised and/or attached to a resolution
are not inversely related. The LDP government and the opposition,
in short, are not playing a zero-sum game. In other words, a higher
approval rate of government-sponsored bills should not be interpreted simply as a reflection of the LDP's bullying tactics in the Diet
or its numerical strength—or to put it in the other way around, a
higher approval rate cannot be accepted hastily as an indication of
failure or ineffectiveness on the part of the opposition.

Why so? Several scholars of Japanese politics have offered explanations. Some argue that in the latter half of the seventies when the
numerical balance between the LDP and the opposition was in equi-
librium, the LDP, anticipating difficulties in managing the Diet process, refrained from pushing through those bills that might provoke

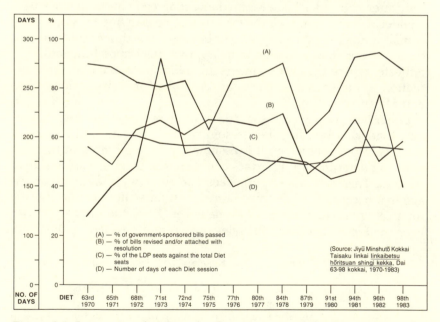

Figure 2.1. Interactions between the Government and the Opposition in the
Diet: 1970–1983

the opposition (Pempel 1974; Iwai 1984; Krauss 1984:284). Others
(Satō and Matsuzaki 1986, 125–28; Iwai 1988, 86–89), in the meantime, suggest that both the quantity and nature of the government-
sponsored (and successfully passed) bills reflect the government's responses to the social and economic needs of the time rather than the
numerical power balance in the Diet.

In addition to these explanations, which take into account a rational side of political behavior and actions as well as formal structures,
it is necessary to explore the meaning and significance of a symbolic
side, or more bluntly, human-as-a-whole-human side, in the legislative process. Infinitely colorful stories and episodes both on and off
the Diet floor that give us an opportunity to peek at broad and complex human interactions among the legislators of all parties have not
been taken seriously as an academically significant subject. There
are, however, things that do not fit rational explanations so comfortably: for instance, why the LDP, despite its numerical superiority to
the opposition, has been so persistently and substantially accommodationist and compromising, whether on the center stage or behind
the scenes, and why it takes so much time for a government-sponsored bill to go through the legislative process under an uninterrupted LDP sole majority government.

As Kōsaka (1967), Kuno (1988), and Yamamoto (1988) testify, even
in the late fifties and early sixties when the country witnessed the
most violent Diet confrontations[4] the opposition and the LDP were,
in fact, acting out the confrontation scenes. And behavior and activities of the members of the Finance Committee, which, as we will see
in detail shortly, are extraordinarily accommodationist in character,
were observed during a period when the LDP maintained the largest
number of seats, 284 of the total 511, in the eight years since December 1972. Or, another example: a noticeable drop of the percentage of
both successfully passed government-sponsored bills and revised
and/or resolution-attached bills in 1979, as shown in figure 2.1, seems
to be explained most convincingly by referring to a severe power
struggle within the LDP at the time that diverted the spiritual as well
as physical energy and resources of the politicians from ordinary Diet
activities (Satō and Matsuzaki 1986, 128).

Mochizuki (1982), in the meantime, offers four reasons why Japan's Diet process needs so much time to pass a bill and makes it
possible for the numerically inferior opposition to exert significant
influence on it. First, the term of Japan's Diet session is shorter than
that of any other advanced democracies, which would help the op-

---

[4] See, for example, Scalapino and Masumi (1962); and Packard (1966).

position win a comparatively easy dismissal of a bill to the limit of time. Second, Japan's bicameral parliament has a comparatively strong second House so the opposition has chances in two places to kill a bill. Third, the standing committee system decentralizes Diet discussions and allows the opposition to delay the process. And fourth, the Japanese custom of seeking unanimity prevents the LDP from bullying to pass a bill that the opposition strongly opposes.

Except for the last point, all of the Mochizuki reasons tend to give us the impression that the system, laws, and rules favor the opposition. Or to put it differently, the opposition counters the government by having recourse to rules and laws. However, not only does numerical superiority allow the ruling LDP, if it so desires, to crush all opposition resistance but the same rules and laws can be used by the government as weapons. For example, in Mochizuki's first point, although it is true that the term of an ordinary Diet session is only 150 days (Secretariat, Diet Law, ARTICLE 10), not only is an extraordinary session regularly convened (usually lasting well over a month) but an ordinary session also can be extended substantially (ART. 12).[5] In the postwar period, there have been seven lengthy (more than 50-days) extensions. The top three were the 1st special Diet in 1947, extended for 154 days; the 71st special Diet in 1972, extended for 130 days; and the 13th ordinary Diet, extended for 85 days (Togawa 1982, 148).

According to Mochizuki's second point, Japan's Diet Law, ART. 59, provides the ruling majority party with favorable conditions. To list one example: although Diet Law, SECTION 4, ART. 59, stipulates that failure by the upper house to reach a final decision within sixty days after receipt of a bill passed by the lower house constitutes a rejection of the bill by the upper house (thus, making a two-thirds majority in the lower house required to reapprove the bill), a sixty-day delay is difficult for the unaligned opposition to achieve. Moreover, for budget approval or the approval required to conclude treaties, a different decision by the upper house or inaction for more than thirty days after receipt will not change the lower house's decision (ARTS. 60, 61).

Laws and rules that aim to prevent delaying tactics exist at many levels of the Diet process. For example, one of the opposition's famous delaying tactics is "cow-walking" (gyūho senjutsu). When voting by open ballot, every member has to cast either a white (for) or blue (against) ballot into the box set at the center of the Diet main hall. The opposition sometimes tries to delay the process in order to

---

[5] For Japanese laws, see Hirano (1983), and for an English translation, Secretariat, House of Representatives (1982).

win a time-out by purposefully walking extremely slowly and with occasional pauses. A veteran Socialist party member testifies that in a recent case, the opposition members tried to keep the one-meter-per-minute pace (Yamamoto 1988, 161–62). However, this tactic can be prevented if the government wishes to rely on the existing rule. The Rules of the House of Representatives, ART. 155-II, unambiguously state that when the Speaker has set a time limit for voting in an open ballot, he may regard those members who did not vote within that time as having abstained from voting.[6]

Despite Mochizuki's third point about decentralization, we see that the law is not in favor of the opposition. Diet Law, ART. 56-III stipulates that a House may, if necessary, call for an interim report by a committee on a pending measure or matter. It also states that the House may, in case of urgent necessity, set a time limit for committee consideration of a measure or matter on which such an interim report has been made or proceed to deliberate it in a plenary sitting. The popularly accepted interpretation of this clause is that it targets the opposition's delaying tactics while a bill is in a standing committee (Kojima 1979).

The fourth point in Mochizuki's list, the Japanese custom of seeking unanimity, is qualitatively different from the other three. Although it appears to be the only truly advantageous point for the numerically inferior opposition, this aspect has not been seriously studied. And it is this aspect that we should explore here instead of simply regarding it as a custom (Satō and Matsuzaki 1986, 125). An open secret in Nagatachō (Japan's counterpart to Capitol Hill) holds that the LDPs and the opposition members have long been and continue to be closely in touch, no matter how furiously they confront each other in public. Countless books and articles—written mostly by journalists who actually have covered the Diet, parties, factions, and politicians for years around-the-clock—contain colorful episodes about closely intertwined relationships among the politicians of both sides.[7]

The following section focuses on the behavior and activities of the members of the Lower House Finance Committee. By viewing them as whole-humans rather than "actors" who represent fragmented

---

[6] For an interpretation of this clause as a preventive measure specifically against the cow-walking tactic, see Kojima (1979, 323).

[7] One of the most trusted such journalist-writers is Togawa Isamu whose works won exceptional confidence among academicians as well as politicians and general audience. See for example, Togawa's eight-volume series that covers postwar politics from 1945 to 1980, Togawa (1980–1981). Also see Thayer (1969, 289–90); Gibney (1975, 277); Krauss (1982, 1984); and Mainichi Shimbunsha (1983).

roles and statuses, special attention will be paid to the members' shared liminal experiences on a number of occasions.

In early July 1981, Finance Committee Chairman Watanuki Tamisuke (LDP) received an unprecedented testimonial from then prime minister, Suzuki Zenkō. Watanuki's Finance Committee in the preceding 94th Diet recorded a 100 percent approval rate for all twenty-one government-proposed bills. As many as seven, or one-third of the bills, were aimed at raising indirect taxes on various items such as liquor and stamps. Because the daily living of ordinary people was likely to be affected by these taxes, all the opposition parties expressed strong criticism of the bills from the outset. It is, therefore, intriguing to examine how the record-breaking achievement was possible by carefully observing interactions and the nature of relationships among the members of the government and the opposition.

Before examining the Watanuki Finance Committee, a brief introduction to the Diet standing committee system is necessary. There are eighteen standing committees in the Lower House and sixteen in the Upper House; in each, the number of members is fixed, although it can be changed by a resolution of the House (Secretariat, Rules of the House of Representatives, ART. 92). Every lower house member must serve on at least one standing committee. Numerical sizes of

TABLE 2.1
Lower House Standing Committees

Committee	Members
Cabinet	30
Local Administration	30
Judicial Affairs	30
Foreign Affairs	30
Finance	40
Education	30
Social and Labor Affairs	40
Agriculture, Forestry, and Fisheries	40
Commerce and Industry	40
Transport	30
Communications	30
Construction	30
Science and Technology	25
Environment	25
Budget	50
Audit	25
Rules and Administration	25
Discipline	20

the parties resulting from each general election determine the number of members each party can send to a standing committee (Diet Law, ART. 46). Members are appointed at the beginning of a session and hold their memberships until their terms of office as members of the Diet expire (Diet Law, ART. 42).

A party's numerical strength also determines whether its member(s) can be included in the board of directors. By tacit agreement, the LDP and the three largest opposition parties put their member(s) on it.[8] In many cases, furthermore, the fourth and numerically smallest opposition party sends a member in the capacity of an observer. All committee have eight directors, except for the committees on Budget (nine directors), Rules and Administration (nine directors) and Discipline (five directors). The off-the-record board of directors' meeting that usually precedes an on-the-record regular committee meeting is much more important decision-making arena than the latter. Every minute of the agenda is decided in detail at the directors' meeting. Thus, participants of a regular committee know in advance who is going to say what, who will raise opposition to the matter and in what order, and how a final agreement will be reached. Neither Diet Laws nor the Rules of the House of Representatives assumes such practices. Obviously, the law rests on the basic assumption that a standing committee's regular meeting is the place for real, not prearranged, discussions. As such, the law refers only briefly to the directors. It is stated that a standing committee shall have one or more directors whose major role is to perform the duties of the chairman when the latter is unable to attend (Rules of the House of Representatives, ART. 38). Laws and rules give exclusive power to the chairman to arrange and maintain order in the committee (ART. 66), to decide the date and time of the committee meeting (ARTS. 67-II, 72), to permit members of a committee to speak, and to decide the length of that time (ART. 45, SEC. 2 and ART. 68, SEC. 1).

Nonetheless, all these matters are decided at the board of directors' meeting. And all decisions must be unanimous. The number of the directors is favorably allocated to the opposition (table 2.2). In other words, outside the formal laws and rules, the opposition maintains a disproportionately firm grip on the core of the decision-making pro-

[8] There were four major opposition parties. Technically, LDP's splinter, the New Liberal Club, could be regarded as the fifth opposition party. Its proximity, however, was such that most scholars, the media and politicians tended to regard the NLC as the one that would eventually revert to the LDP. And they proved to be right in August 1986.

Where the number of a standing committee's members is less than twenty, only the two largest opposition parties are entitled to have directors' posts.

TABLE 2.2
Numerical Strength of the Parties and Allocation of the Finance Committee
Memberships and Directorships as of August 1980

	Number of Members	Percentage of Diet Seats	Percentage of Committee Members	Percentage of Directors
LDP[a]	286	55.97	57.5 (23)[b]	50.0 (4)
JSP	106	20.74	22.5 (9)	25.0 (2)
Kōmeitō	34	6.65	7.5 (3)	12.5 (1)
DSP	33	6.46	5.0 (2)	12.5 (1)
JCP	29	5.67	5.0 (2)	0.0 (observer)
NLC	12	2.35	2.5 (1)	0.0
SDL	3	0.59	0.0	0.0
Independents	8	1.57	0.0	0.0
Total	511	100.00	100.00 (40)	100.0 (8)

Source: Miyagawa (1980, 146–51, 232).

[a] LDP = Liberal Democratic Party; JSP = Japan Socialist party; Kōmeitō = Clean Government party; DSP = Democratic Socialist party; JCP = Japan Communist party; NLC = New Liberal Club; SDL = Social Democratic League.

[b] The figures in parentheses are actual numbers of the members.

cess in the Diet. This is one of the most significant examples in which informal, more egalitarian arrangements are well institutionalized by either ignoring laws and rules or giving them outrageously stretched interpretations.

It was of utmost importance to Chairman Watanuki at the outset to build good human relationships among the committee members in order to make smooth management possible. It is popularly held in Nagatachō that the best committee chairs are those who are good at informal, behind-the-scenes negotiations based on their strong ties with members of both the opposition and the LDP. A committee chair who is interested only in policies is often a target of criticisms that imply incompetence.[9] Indeed, the need and importance of human relationships are concepts so deeply held by the Diet members of both the LDP and the opposition that well-institutionalized, twice-a-year informal get-together parties are hosted by the speaker and vice-speaker of each House and by each standing committee chair. Expenses for these parties are covered by the Diet budget.[10] The committee members take an overseas group trip usually during the sum-

[9] For one such example, see a Budget Committee chairman in the 101st special Diet in 1984, "Onkō iinchō" (1984).

[10] Mainichi Shimbun, Aug. 30, 1983, p. 3.

mer recess of the Diet. This so-called study mission is participated in by well over one hundred, sometimes more than two hundred, Diet members annually. It costs 170 million yen for the lower house and nearly 100 million yen (approximately $1 U.S. = 234 yen) for the upper house each year.[11] A sixteen-day trip to Southeast Asia and Oceania was organized for the Watanuki committee. The group visited leading officials of banks and stock exchange markets in Hong Kong, Thailand, Singapore, and Australia from mid-August to early September. For two or three weeks, a group places itself in the midst of foreign cultures where their familiar, taken-for-granted views and beliefs are shaken and become subject to reexamination. A leveling mood overwhelms the members. Travel, especially overseas travel, provides an extraordinarily fitting situation for participants to reflect upon themselves while loosening the guard over their individual Selves. Like a transitional ritual, participants go through a three-phase process (V. Turner 1977, 94): they are physically and mentally detached from their earlier fixed points in the social structure and cultural stereotypes; consequently, they are overwhelmed by ambiguities and uncertainties; and then they restore new states of meaningful consistency by incorporating new elements under a new organizational principle. This process allows a situation in which members together can transcend roles, statuses, and other institutional arrangements of nomos and build whole-human-to-whole-human relationships with each other.

During the 93d extraordinary Diet in early autumn 1980, the Watanuki committee organized what they called a "Seeing Committee" (*me de miru iinkai*) or "Moving Committee" (*ugoku iinkai*), on Wednesdays. Anticipating that in the coming 94th ordinary Diet they would have many more bills to handle than any other committee and that the subjects of these bills would include stocks, indirect taxes on alcohol products, and issuance of new coins, the committee in a group visited the Tokyo Stock Exchange, a beer factory, the Mint Bureau, the Bank of Japan's underground strongroom, and a customs office in the neighboring port city, Yokohama.

Moving Committee activities helped members gradually nurture a feeling of mutual friendship among themselves through a series of such shared experiences as tasting freshly tapped beer in a beer factory, touching and smelling newly printed bank notes in the Mint Bureau, stepping deep into the tightly guarded Bank of Japan's underground strongroom, and rambling around the exotic old port city's customs office.

[11] *Mainichi Shimbun*, Aug. 28, 1983, p. 3.

In mid-November, Watanuki, like many other committee chairmen, hosted a get-together party. Usually, such a party is held at a hotel in buffet style. His committee, however, chose a Japanese-style room so that everyone could take off his shoes and sit cross-legged side by side on a Japanese *tatami* (straw mat) floor in a very relaxing manner. When Japanese take off their shoes and sit closely on the same, low level, they feel a significantly intensified sense of camaraderie. This is especially so when they eat and drink there together. Experiences of these series of shared moments of informal bonding soon helped the committee members come close enough to be called by others "Committee of Buddies" (*nakayoshi iinkai*).[12]

The substantial discussions of the 94th ordinary Diet started in late January 1981. The Finance Committee's first major discussion was over the government-sponsored bill that, if enacted, would put broader and heavier indirect taxes on alcoholic products, ranging from beer, wine, and sake to powdered spirits. The bill was aimed at increasing tax revenue to cover the country's ballooning budget deficit.[13]

All other parties strongly opposed the bill. Their main argument was that it was simplistic and short-sighted to raise taxes to cover the deficit without making a full-scale effort to achieve fundamental changes in the tax system and structural reform of the entire administrative system so as to cut the spending drastically. They pointed out that the deficit burden was unfairly put on ordinary people's shoulders because beer, wine, whiskey, and sake were popular beverages among the general public. The opposition also noted that a price rise on such popular products as beer and sake would trigger an overall consumer price increase.[14]

The headquarters of the opposition parties, therefore, instructed their respective directors on the Finance Committee to confront Watanuki with three demands before they agreed to sit at the board of directors' meeting. The demands included: (1) the bill should be treated as "an important bill" (*jūyōhōan*). According to the Diet Law, ART. 56-II, such a bill is submitted to the House plenary sitting for explanation of its purport (technically, any bill can be defined as "an important bill" when the committee on Rules and Administration deems it necessary); (2) A pertinent state minister, in this case, the Finance minister, should always be present at the committee meet-

[12] "Kon Kokkai o Kaerimite" (1981, 3).

[13] In the 1981 fiscal year, the government had to rely on the issuance of public bonds for as much as 26 percent of its budget (*Oriental Wave* 1[Sept. 1982]: 17–19).

[14] For the detailed argument of each party, including the LDP government and makers of beer, wine, and sake, see Shūgiin Jimukyoku (1981, pts. 1–8).

ings to answer questions as well as to explain the purport of a gov-ernment-sponsored bill at the start of discussion (neither law nor rule requires a state minister to do so); and (3) committee meetings should not be held in the evening (no such time limit clause is found in the laws or rules). The opposition, citing the recent deaths of two mem-bers of the Finance committee (a JSP and a DSP), told Watanuki that nothing was more important than health and that evening sessions were too stressful. In addition, the opposition headquarters replaced their directors with ordinary committee members. That is, one JSP director with whom Watanuki had worked since the previous term became an ordinary member of the committee so that a new JSP member could take a director's post. The Kōmeitō did the same.

Not only was camaraderie undermined, which had been growing among the directors, but chances of direct face-to-face communica-tion were considerably reduced because of the intervention from party headquarters. Watanuki's gravest worry at that time was not the conflicting stance of the opposition but the member changes on the board of directors. In other words, the paucity and uncertainty of direct communication with the directors of the opposition parties made him "feel as if [he] . . . was helplessly standing in front of a house whose entrance [he] . . . was unable to find."[15]

What is significant here to our theoretical point of view is that a steadily built camaraderie among directors—the success of which can be attributed at least partly to Chairman Watanuki's initiatives and efforts—worked in favor of the opposition rather than the LDP gov-ernment. Although Chairman Watanuki, a member of the majority LDP government, could actually pass the bill through recourse either to the numerical strength of his party or to Diet laws and rules, he did not. As a matter of fact, such formal, legal means were the last thing on his mind. Instead of simply dismissing the opposition's re-quests as unreasonable or legally groundless, Watanuki took them with utmost seriousness and made desperate efforts to satisfy them.[16]

---

[15] *Toyama Shimbun*, Feb. 1981, p. 3.

[16] To reemphasize, what is involved is not intimidation or conspiracy. Diet members feel it is mutual trust: "What is agreed upon shall be kept among themselves even if it meets opposition from their own party" (" 'Dakyōgeki' no kurogo" 1983). See also the very similar statements gathered by Krauss (1984, 271–78) through his interviews with Diet members and the accounts of the veteran members, Yamamoto (1988) and Kuno (1988). All of them testify that this is an absolutely essential and common characteristic of those members of both the opposition and the LDP who are respected for their ability in Diet management. Krauss (1984, 275) describes this trait as "having the abil-ity to transcend one's own party's view." And a number of Diet members and their

During the first week of February, Watanuki worked hard to obtain an approval from the committee on Rules and Administration for the alcohol tax bill's *important* status. He succeeded. It was also arranged that the finance minister's explanation of the bill at the plenary sitting would be on February 12. Directors of the opposition now were ready to begin an off-the-record board of directors' meeting. And once it begins, a formal committee meeting should be expected to have few troubles. At that moment, Watanuki, with a sigh of relief, said, "I feel . . . I . . . could finally find an entrance."[17] From the first regular meeting day, the committee started full-scale discussions. At the start, the opposition made one more request. At the next committee meeting, they wished to call upon witnesses representing manufacturers of wine, beer, and sake. The request was approved. During the next two consecutive meetings, representatives of six makers of alcohol products and one university professor of economics testified.

Of the other conditions requested by the opposition—that is, that the finance minister should always be present and meetings ought not to be extended into evening—the former was almost perfectly kept. Even though Minister Watanabe Michio once or twice came late or left the room for a short while, he attended every committee meeting on the alcohol tax bill. Avoidance of evening hours was also realized. The latest meeting during the bill's discussion closed at 7:24 P.M., the only one that went beyond 7:00 P.M. It took one full-day and three half-day sessions to complete discussions and to hear testimony concerning the bill. The chairman pronounced the close of the discussion over the bill on the afternoon of February 24.

The next morning, a board of directors' meeting was held. Watanuki suggested that to have a modest "wine-tasting gathering" (*kikizakekai*) by all committee members the following evening would be an appropriate conclusion of the discussion over the alcohol bill. Watanuki shrewdly reminded the members of the remarks of some of the witnesses from sake makers during the testimony to the effect that the Japanese sake makers recently had been improving their product so that it not only had a superior taste but also would not cause either hangovers or diabetes. This would be a good opportunity, he added invitingly, to better appreciate the country's traditional alcoholic beverage, which was being threatened by the increasing popularity of beer and wine. All members applauded the idea promptly. In addition to nine kinds of sake and beer from five makers who had testi-

secretaries, including Watanuki, made almost identical remarks during my casual conversations with them.

17 *Toyama Shimbun*, Feb. 8, 1981, p. 3.

fied before the committee, Finance Minister Watanabe offered to con-
tribute one of his favorite brands of sake brewed in his constituency.
The place was set in the neighboring memorial hall, Ozaki Kensei
Kinenkan, named after the father of constitutional politics, Ozaki
Gakudō, just across the street from the Diet building, instead of a
luxury entertainment spot in downtown Tokyo.

On the evening of the following day, Watanuki hosted the kikizakekai, which, not surprisingly, turned into a merry drinking party.
Even the Communist party members, who, on principle, would not
join informal dining/drinking parties with the LDPs, came this time.
Both the official purpose and the place were perfectly acceptable to
the Communist party as well as to other more flexible opposition
party members. One of the Communist party members who usually
was rather straitlaced and stuffy revealed his love of sake a little too
much in that melting atmosphere, according to Watanuki's first political secretary, Kawashima Kyūichi, who was also there. Everyone
readily took off his formal mask under the enchantingly absorbing
influence of sake. As a number of scholars of Japanese society have
observed (Embree 1939, 209; Dore 1958, 208; Plath 1964, 87–88; Edwards 1982, 703), drinking parties in the Japanese setting effectively
create and strengthen a sense of unity among the participants. That
is, drinking sake, like a vast range of other liminal experiences, helps
us slip out of the conscious, norm-governed world of nomos: we are
carried away into a liminal phase where a utilitarian principle is overpowered by the spontaneous, egalitarian, whole-human-to-whole-
human relationship; we together transcend the temporarily invalidated institutional arrangements of nomos, and we transcend our
own Selves as well.

Nobody cared to describe the differences among the various kinds
of sake and beer presented. Like other committee members, Watanuki said afterwards that he could not discern much difference at all
but enjoyed most the sake contributed by Finance Minister Watanabe
Michio. No one actually had believed in the first place that they were
going to just "taste wine." It is safe, therefore, to assume that by then
the members' perception of formal roles, institutional arrangements,
and principles had been modified to the degree that nomos structures no longer appeared absolute to them—that is, subject to their
flexible interpretations and management.

The next morning, the committee put the alcohol tax bill to a vote.
All members were present, and each opposition representative, according to the rule, explained why his party opposed the bill. LDP
committee members, excluding the chairman, accounted for twenty-
two, a majority of the forty-member committee. Support by more

than one-half of the members present will give a bill approval. In a tie, the chairman's vote becomes decisive (Diet Law, ART. 50). At the request of Chairman Watanuki for a stand-up vote of support, all of the LDP representatives—and they alone—registered approval of the bill. This response was known and accepted well in advance by opposition members.

Watanuki and the directors already had completed detailed talks to build a common satisfactory ground. They had agreed that approval of the government-proposed alcohol products tax bill would be allowed by the opposition with no active obstructionism (e.g., meeting boycott). At the same time, it was decided that a resolution sponsored by all six political parties (i.e., cosponsored by the LDP as well as JSP, Kōmeitō, DSP, JCP, and NLC) should be attached to the bill. The resolution contained the following provisions: (1) to fundamentally reform the alcohol products tax system, broader studies should be undertaken; (2) minor Japanese sake makers would receive legal as well as administrative support to survive; and (3) the enactment of this bill ought not to trigger a general consumer price rise, and for that reason, the government should provide careful guidance.[18] The opposition's requests, points of view and basic principles were thus substantially taken into the bill and will influence the future course of administration because resolutions exert political binding power.[19]

As a representative of the six cosponsors of the resolution, a JSP director read aloud to the committee an explanation of the purport of the resolution. The entire committee approved at once with applause. Finance Minister Watanabe who was present then asked the chairman to allow him to speak. As the pertinent minister of the government, he gave assurance that the government would follow the principles of the resolution.[20]

It is intriguing to notice the stark contrast between the ostensible formal *fact*—that is, as shown in the official record, the passage of the alcohol products tax bill solely by the LDP's majority votes with all five opposition parties opposed to it[21]—and what really took place, as revealed by our examination. The officially recorded fact cannot help but give the impression that the LDP, by recourse to its numerical strength and Diet laws, bullied to pass the bill, although it took a considerable time given the opposition's resistance. Nonetheless, the reality was totally different. It is especially significant that the attached resolution was cosponsored by the LDP, not just the oppo-

---

[18] Shūgiin Jimukyoku, 1981, pt. 8 (Feb. 27, 1981), p. 3.

[19] On the binding political effect of a resolution, see Kojima (1979, 307).

[20] Shūgiin Jimukyoku, 1981, pt. 8 (Feb. 27, 1981), p. 4.

[21] Jiyū Minshutō Kokkai Taisaku Iinkai, 1981, SEC. 2, p. 5.

sition alone. This fact ensured that the government would not ignore the resolution that incorporated substantially the opposition's views and interests.

Discussion

We have seen that nearly all the opposition's requests—which had no legal grounds and, hence, could have been easily rejected—were met. Personal relationships among the committee members, especially among the directors of the LDP and the opposition, seem to have provided an essential condition for this to occur. The committee members repeatedly slipped out of nomos into a liminal phase through a series of shared liminal experiences: an overseas group trip; a day's excursion as a Moving Committee to such unusual places as the heavily guarded underground strongroom of the Bank of Japan and a beer factory; a party in which everyone went barefoot and sat, ate, and drank together on the Japanese tatami floor; and an ever-merrier "wine-tasting" party. Cumulatively, they provided the condition in which a whole-human-to-whole-human relationship could be built. And that, in turn, makes it possible for the members to transcend party lines, boundaries of roles, statuses, laws, and ideological categories. As a consequence, these formal arrangements of nomos begin to appear arbitrary or invalid to them and hence capable of being relativized or ignored.

Chairman Watanuki Tamisuke, for instance, came to be popularly called by his first name, Tami-san, or even more amicably, Tami-chan, instead of by his formal title, Mr. Chairman, Watanuki. Western cultures, in general, allow first names among adults who are not very close to each other. However, such familiarity is not as common in Japan. When opposition members identifies themselves as adversaries of the LDP government, here symbolized by Chairman Watanuki Tamisuke, they would likely call Watanuki, "Watanuki iinchō" (Mr. Chairman, Watanuki). In contrast, when such a definition of roles begins to appear invalid to them, they may well feel that Tami-san is more natural. The committee, especially the directors, came to call each other by amicable names. Regardless of their party membership, they came to feel natural enough to pat each other's shoulders, to have a little chat while standing in the hallway whenever they ran into one another, or to have a little longer talk at a modest coffee shop in the Diet building.

When the identification of Self and others is modified, attitudes and relationship should change accordingly. Already, in early February, Watanuki actually asked the directors to persuade their respective headquarters not to interfere. In other words, he asked the directors to make every effort to neutralize their parties' attempts at overturning what had been agreed upon among the directors.[22] What this suggests is that a broader context was defined as consisting of *we*, the committee on this side, and *they*, the party headquarters on the other. To put it differently, at least in the perception of Watanuki and the directors, the context was no longer the one in which a board of directors was split into adversaries, each of whom represented, and was closely instructed by, their respective party headquarters.

The perception and definition of the issues, party interests, and their priority may also alter. For instance, in the case of the alcohol products tax bill, the opposition shifted its emphasis from attacking the bill as a threat to the ordinary citizens' daily living to reducing the bill's possible negative effects. In the meantime, the LDP members' attitudes were modified as well. They came to be willing to incorporate the opposition's proposal that, among other things, more far-sighted, fundamental reform of the tax system on alcohol products should be given priority. This is the prerequisite for the preconsultation and negotiation made possible at board of directors' meeting, which, in turn, is the prerequisite for the formal, on-the-record committee meeting.

The process of change at the perception level seems to involve inevitably a loss of clarity and absoluteness of the existing classification of people, things, and principles. A whole context is deformed even in the Diet. The Diet represents the chief embodiment of nomos order. Roles and statuses are clearly defined, and activities proceed according to the formal rules of the Diet. Each participant is expected to play the formal political roles. Laws are written upon this basic assumption. A whole political system is based on this assumption. However, intrusions of the liminal domains constantly bring in, even here, ambiguities and inconsistencies. In short, even at the center of nomos, deformation can take place to the degree that political and legal codes appear to the Diet members, the core bearers of the nomos structures, as invalid, or, at least, not carrying sufficient legitimacy to be strictly maintained in actuality. This deformed state, in turn, offers the essential condition for free rearrangement and reordering of any and every element, old and new, of nomos to become possible.

The practices in Japan's Diet, as described so far, may well be seen as a fairly radical disregard and disdain for the existing political, legal system because these practices are engaged in by the chief holders of

---

[22] *Toyama Shimbun*, Feb. 8, 1981, p. 3; ibid., Feb. 1, 1981, p. 3.

the system themselves. They almost actively ignore the existing laws, rules, and the formal institutional arrangements. Instead, we have seen them eagerly and freely adopt more flexible means. This adaptation is possible because of the fluidity even at the core of the structures of nomos. This fluidity would allow the Diet members to question and transcend any existing institutional arrangements. Most importantly, individuals or groups do not intend actions to transcend and slight laws, roles, and institutions to attain a certain objective. On the contrary, these are the activities that are naturally induced by the condition of structural fluidity. These practices, in other words, have nothing, at the bottom, to do with human's calculations. They are far more deeply rooted in the human three-dimensional worldview, too far beyond human conscious control.

It is a popularly held view among scholars and journalists that the financially resourceful LDP government throws money to the opposition members in various ways—giving them hard cash under such names as traditional obituary gifts, compassionate gifts for illness, wedding gifts, and the like, and inviting them to expensive dinner parties or to golf or mahjong matches where the LDPs purposefully let the opposition members win so that they can be given cash prizes.[23]

To emphasize only a calculated transactional aspect of a deed, however, may prevent us from realizing the significance it carries in its entirety. What is involved in such informal occasions as dining and drinking or golfing and playing mahjong should not be taken simply as calculated deals. Some money may actually be involved. Yet, it is used more often to help create the moments in which people share the experiences of liminality rather than to buy unilaterally a specific result or a more vague, general compliance. It seems to be much more appropriate to interpret this kind of ubiquitously observed behavior and activity in politics as well as in society at large not solely from a rational choice perspective but from the point of view that takes a symbolic, human-as-a-whole-human side into account.

The Watanuki committee dealt with a total of twenty-one government-sponsored bills. As many as seventeen were revised or emerged with an attached resolution to incorporate the opposition's views and interests. Of the remaining four, one was a unanimously approved farm aid bill that all parties were willing to support from the outset. The rest of the bills were backed by all but the Communist

---

[23] See, for example, Thayer (1969, 289–90); Gendai Seiji Mondai Kenkyūkai (1973, 293–97), Gibney (1975, 277); Mainichi Shimbunsha (1983); and Nagata (1983, 42–53).

party. In other words, here the government's supposed 100 percent success actually constituted an 85.7 percent merger of all parties. The average of all lower house standing committees between the 63d special Diet in 1970 and the 98th ordinary Diet in 1983 was 82.68 percent and 60.03 percent, respectively. So the Watanuki committee represents an extreme case, although it reflects a general pattern of interactions between the two sides.

Indeed, the significant influence the opposition exerts on the country's basic policy courses deserves more serious attention. A few points of view attribute Japan's conspicuous political flexibility, at least in part, to the LDP's adoption of the opposition's policies.[24] Well-known examples of such flexibility include successfully dealing with the problems of pollution,[25] the smooth transformation of the industrial structure, and the realization of an advanced welfare system.[26]

Such a degree of merging between the dominant LDP, with greater resources and overpowering numbers, and the opposition, with fewer resources and ununited, seems to be attainable mostly because of the fluidity of nomos made available through the members' ubiquitous, informal, nonpolitical behavior and activities rather than formal structures and intentional political actions.

The Meaning of an Election: Stranger-king, Native Son, and Symbolic Rejuvenation of the Community

The preceding section examined a merger in horizontal relationships at the level of national politics, that is, a merger among the groups of political elites. Such a merger, however, is by no means exclusive to horizontal relationships. Because an intrusion of a liminal domain is indiscriminate and ubiquitous, structural fluidity would be possible anywhere. Therefore, whether it is a horizontal or vertical relationship should make no difference. Both have an equal vulnerability to the intrusions and overpowering of liminality. The concrete vertical relationship between a political elite and the voters during an election campaign is our next focus of attention.

During an election campaign, in many cultures, an extraordinary state of excitement dominates an entire community. The occasion of-

---

[24] Ōtake (1983); "JSP's Decline" (1986).

[25] Pempel (1982, chap. 6), Hershkowitz and Salerni (1987).

[26] Nakagawa Y. (1979, 2). See also Pempel (1982) and Curtis and Ishikawa (1984) for a discussion of higher degree of receptivity, responsiveness, and flexibility in Japanese politics.

fers a careful observer an ideal opportunity to see liminal domain intrude into and overpower nomos temporally and spatially. In the orgiastic atmosphere of an election campaign, people of the community have a rich opportunity to reactivate their reflexivity to reexamine themselves and their relationships with the candidate. An election is an opportunity for a community to collectively experience communitas, that is, symbolic inversion. An election symbolically rejuvenates the entire community as well as individual members and their relationships with others. The following section tries to interpret the meaning of an election to the people of the community as well as to a candidate and to the community as a whole. The case is chosen from a national election in contemporary Japan. The focus of the analysis is on the occurrences at the campaign headquarters of one LDP Diet member.

Election campaigning in contemporary Japan is a manifestation of an extraordinary occasion of ritual exchanges that involves ordinary people, on the one hand, and an elite politician, on the other. It is an opportunity for a symbolic exchange/merger between a candidate and the voters. During the election campaign, ordinarily remote national level politics, (Massey 1975) in which people are regarded en masse as the individually faceless *public* or *voters* is drawn into the people's daily lives. Every voter now appears as an individual with an articulate personality, preferences, and concerns. This inversion of ordinary political life during the election campaign is most vividly observed at a candidate's campaign headquarters. There everyone is in a state of excitement in an orgiastic atmosphere throughout a fifteen-day period.[27]

Although Japanese election campaigning has been studied by scholars[28] almost no scholar seriously studies what is happening at a campaign headquarters. The focus of studies and analyses is placed instead exclusively on a candidate's strategies, people's voting behavior, political issues, role and influence of media, and so forth. Consequently, the candidate and voters appear as the exploiter-manipulator versus the exploited-manipulated, or vice versa.[29] Some describe their relationship as reciprocal.[30] Either way, the underlying assumption is similar to that of the popular exchange theory or patron-client perspective.

[27] For more on the orgiastic aspect, see, for example, S. Oda (1982, 67–68).

[28] For example, Curtis (1971).

[29] Ishida (1961, 85–102, 227–35); Matsushita (1962, 127–43), Yoshimura (1964, 216–26) and Fukutake (1971, 223–54);

[30] Fukuoka (1983); Curtis and Ishikawa (1984).

Exchange theory proponents[31] and those who hold the patron-client perspective[32] share the basic assumption that those who are less well endowed will necessarily be dominated by those who possess more; or to put it differently, that A who receives from B must be indebted to B, while B feels legitimate, direct control over A.

The structuralist perspective, in the meantime, suggests "exchange" in a broader, fuller context. As Ueno (1981) points out, possession does not by itself lend prestige or legitimacy of rule to a possessor. Only by giving possessions to others and thereby mobilizing interactions among members of the society, she argues, is one able to gain prestige. Society consists, after all, of networks of interactions and relations. "No interaction" means the nonexistence of society. It is a whole system of networks of exchange that lends prestige or legitimacy of rule to a giver. Through various ritual exchanges, the audience may confer maximal or minimal prestige on a giver, or it may deprive a giver of it altogether. That is, prestige in the system is given to the person through the sanction of the audience in ritual exchanges (Ueno 1981, 103).

By taking this perspective, we assign greater significance to those who possess less to exchange and lay greater emphasis on the merger and complementarity between giver and recipient. For example, we would not interpret a situation in which a candidate throws a drinking party for a group of constituents as an attempt to buy specific votes or their general support. Such an interpretation would be, as Sahlins (1976), Polanyi (1966), or Polanyi, Arensberg, and Pearson (1957) might say, a copy of the thinking behind the capitalist market economy; to think that includes no anthropology.

An alternative approach demands that we pay major attention to how exchanges take place rather than how much is exchanged. The context and process of exchange, instead of the result, are the focus of analysis. How ritual exchange proceeds and how the audience sanctions it will be our main interests.

Stranger-king and Native Son

An election can be seen as an occasion for the creation or re-creation of candidate-voter bonds through ritual exchange. Sahlins' recent efforts to reconcile structuralist wisdom with history offer a useful suggestion about how to analyze cases in which two forces collide with

---

[31] For example, Homans (1950, 1958); Gouldner (1960); Blau (1964, 1968); and Befu (1974).

[32] Ike (1972, 1977); Schmidt (1977).

each other and then, through ritual exchanges in liminality, merge to produce a new structure. Sahlins (1981, 1983) takes cases from Fiji, Hawaii, and some small native communities that faced the advent of a foreign ruler, the *stranger-king*. They managed to "domesticate" (Sahlins 1981, 127) him so that his dangerous, destructive elements were kept under control while his fresh, regenerative force was taken for the benefit of their communities.[33]

Sahlins suggested that the contents of categories in the structural classification changed. That is, Sahlins added a progressive temporal change to the Lévi-Straussian structuralism that is inherently ahistorical. The destructive as well as creative stranger-king was an outsider at first but, through marriage with a sacrificial indigenous woman, became the community's ruler. To look at this process from the other way around, the dual-natured stranger-king was "domesticated" by marriage to a native woman. The community gained fresh, regenerative blood from the stranger-king. Moreover, he and his sons were incorporated into his wife's lineage (i.e., matrilineal lineage vis-à-vis patrilineal lineage, which is formal and dominant in the community). In short, the creative as well as destructive stranger-king changed his position in the structural classification from *outside* to *margin*. He must be situated at the margin. His role as a ruler is to mediate between the outside world and the community. He embodies female as well as male and outside as well as inside. This dualism is essential for him to be a legitimate ruler; yet this inherent dualism keeps him at the margin because a full-fledged community member never would have such dualism.

The relationship between candidates and the voters of their constituencies may be viewed in this framework. Candidates need not be newcomers. Those who attempt reelection would go through basically the same ritual to secure themselves as "representatives" of their communities. Indeed, as Sahlins (1981) notes, the same symbolic process takes place at a coronation ritual—that is, reenactment of the original scenes of the advent and incorporation of the stranger-king. Japan's fifteen-day election campaign period may be viewed either as an original scene of the advent-incorporation of the stranger-king or a ritualized reenactment of it. Through these rituals, candidates become "the representatives" of their communities, while the community "domesticates" and accepts them as "the representatives" who mediate between the outside world and the community for the latter's benefit.

[33] Sahlins' interpretation is inspired by the work of Clastres (1977).

The Meaning of an Election

Participatory observation for this study was conducted during the December 3–17, 1983 general election campaigning period at the incumbent Liberal Democrat, Watanuki Tamisuke's, headquarters. His constituency, Tokaoka city of Toyama prefecture, is located in snowy northwest Japan, about a four-hour train ride from Tokyo. As mentioned, because studies and analyses of election strategies and voter behavior have been done already by a number of scholars, my focus will be on the election as an orgiastic occasion of symbolic inversion, on collective reflexivity, and on ritual exchange.

In his successful previous elections, Watanuki set his campaign headquarters in one of Takaoka's largest Buddhist temples. The practical reason for the choice was the space that the temple could provide to accommodate a large campaign staff and numerous visitors. An equally important reason was the symbolic importance of that particular Buddhist temple as a lucky charm, as the number of Watanuki's victory celebrations at the temple headquarters increased. Thus one of the most important tasks for his staff in the precampaign period was to secure their *good-luck* (*engi no yoi*) headquarters. Buddhist temples are overwhelmingly preferred to modern office buildings by Japanese candidates, regardless of their party membership, not only as campaign headquarters but also as places for campaign speeches before local audiences. (Watanuki, like his competitors, averaged five speeches daily.)

In Japan's midsize, multicandidate electoral district system, usually more than three candidates run for the Diet seats in one district. Watanuki was among five candidates (three Liberal Democrats, one Socialist, and one Communist) who competed for the three seats of the Second District in Toyama. All of them used Buddhist temples extensively. The people can gather there, take off their shoes, and sit together on the tatami (straw-mat) floor of a sparsely furnished room. Unlike modern offices, or lecture halls, there are no chairs and no authoritative-looking platform for a speaker. Instead, there are scattered floor pillows (*zabuton*) for the audience and speaker alike, with a couple of heaters in winter. In short, what a Buddhist temple provides is not just a meeting place but an atmosphere, where ritual exchange and orgiastic inversion between a candidate and the people are possible. To secure a Buddhist temple for a campaign headquarters and local campaign speeches is, thus, of crucial importance. It is not merely a matter of size or convenient location; it is, more importantly, how well these places are suited as settings for ritual exchanges.

The campaign can start only after the headquarters is turned symbolically into an extraordinary space through rituals. All five candidates of the Toyama-2 district performed a headquarters-opening ritual (*Jimusho Biraki*). This ritual began with the candidates' visits to their favorite Shinto shrines or their mentors' graves. Then followed the *Shutsujinshiki* (an archaic term used in the Middle Ages by warriors, which refers to the ritual performed before going into battle); this ritual was sometimes accompanied by the beating of a war drum (*jindaiko*) or the making of rice cakes with traditional wooden pestles and mortars (*mochitsuki*).[34]

Symbolically, the Shutsujinshiki marks the discontinuation of ordinary time and space and an entry into an extraordinary phase. Every candidate then puts on a pair of white gloves, a large white ribbon-flower on the left lapel of his suit, and a wide white sash, just like a cordon, with his name brush-stroked in glossy black *sumi* ink on it. He wears these throughout the campaign period. Such accoutrements, which look quite strange in ordinary time and space, are popularly seen as symbols of the purity of a candidate's personality.[35] However, these otherwise strange trappings can also be interpreted as symbols of a candidate's out-of-ordinary state of being during the campaigning.

The Shutsujinshiki may be regarded as an occasion in which a candidate, the *stranger-king*, symbolically declares his advent to the constituency. Like Sahlins's stranger-king, candidates could be beneficial as well as harmful to constituencies. They might, for example, use their legislative power to harm the welfare of the people. Yet, at the same time, they could bring benefits to constituencies by exercising their legislative power. A candidate tries to become "the representative" of the constituency just as the stranger-king tried to become the ruler of the community. The constituencies, in the face of the candidates' advent, try to "domesticate" them to keep their dangerous potential under control. In the case of the stranger-king, a sacrificial indigenous woman was used to incorporate the stranger-king into an inferior matrilineal lineage in the community. A modern Japanese political candidate is incorporated into various kinds of professional and private associations as well as formal and informal personal networks—that is, the candidate becomes an honorary head of a number of organizations, such as a public bath owners' association and a neighborhood baseball team.[36]

[34] For each candidate's Shutsujinshiki, see *Toyama Shimbun* Dec. 4, 1983, p.3.

[35] For the symbolic meaning of white gloves, see Ohnuki-Tierney (1984, 30).

[36] On this aspect, see Yoshimura (1964, 223–26); Curtis (1971, chaps. 5, 7); and Fukutake (1971, 227–232).

How does such incorporation become possible between candidates and the people of their constituencies? It is not simply the result of the candidates' clever strategies or short-sightedness (Fukutake 1971, 228) or apathy (Ishida 1961, 91) on the part of the people, especially those in rural areas.[37] How people come to accept them as the honorary heads of their circles—that is, at least nominally, as superior, if not full-fledged, members of their circles or communities—has seldom been seriously questioned. To find an answer, we need to examine the very beginning of the encounter between a candidate and the constituency. A careful study of the occurrences during an election campaign is important.

Watanuki's campaign headquarters had a tatami-floored main hall where all his staff sat along plain wooden low tables that were arranged in a U-shape along the walls. Originally, each person's place was loosely fixed; however, even that order gradually disappeared, especially in the latter half of the fifteen-day campaign period, and anyone sat in any place at any time. By simply placing more floor pillows (zabuton) along the table, the number of people, too, was never fixed. With tables set along the walls, enough space was left in the center to welcome anyone to sit cross-legged around a couple of heaters for hours to chat, sip tea, and consume abundant snacks like candies, rice crackers, and mandarin oranges. A smaller room next to the main hall was also equipped with two long, low tables to function as a dining room. All the staff and the candidate as well as the candidate's family members ate lunch and dinner together while sitting on a tatami floor.

Visitors, too, were invited to eat anytime within the meal time (about three hours each for lunch and dinner). Menus of the buffet-style meals were humble, simple, and conventional, but there was always abundant food, which was served warm. Housewives who belonged to a Watanuki support group cooked in a large kitchen of the temple. They also kept abundant tea and snacks available for the staff and visitors.[38] The atmosphere of the campaign headquarters was always festival-like, filled with excitement. Not one minute of silence existed. People in a number of small, unorganized, and shifting groups talked or argued different things at the same time. The *New York Times* journalist, Clyde Haberman (1986) described another

[37] This view, implicitly or explicitly, is persistently held. See Ishida (1961, 86–91, 166–69, 185–89, 228–32); Matsushita (1962, 131–43, 148–52, 224–30); and Fukutake (1971, 227–33).

[38] For the festival-like abundance and nondiscriminating service of meals and snacks at election campaign headquarters in general, see *Yomiuri Shimbun*, Dec. 15, 1983, p. 9; *Asahi Shimbun*, Dec. 16, 1983.

headquarters as "a session of gossip and green tea." It was too noisy, and there were too many visitors (some of them total strangers to the campaign staff) for serious staff meetings to be held concerning campaign strategies or to analyze and assess the on-going situation.

From early morning until late at night, staff and visitors alike never left the snacks and tea. They chatted about anything, election-related or not—their children, grandchildren, popular television programs, rival candidates, and stories of past elections. Watanuki and his wife, son, and daughters were no different from the others. As Oda (1982, 67–68) notes, it was the time when differences of socioeconomic status in ordinary life disappeared or were even inverted in an orgiastic atmosphere. Watanuki ate the same food and sipped the same tea that everyone at the headquarters had. He had no private room, not even a separate corner or desk of his own.

Campaign strategies—such as discussions concerning to which local areas he should travel, with whom he should meet, and before whom he should make campaign speeches (his wife, son, or daughter sometimes substituted for him)—were not decided by Watanuki. As he himself noted, he liked to campaign according to the plan given to him. He said, "I am confident. I need not worry about a thing." The plan was not the product of organized strategy meetings. Rather, members of various support groups—some based on occupations, religion, hobbies, and so forth, and others on geographical areas—made suggestions and requests about campaign plans at the headquarters. For example, a Takaoka area women's support group was notably active among Watanuki's many support groups. They carried out an almost autonomous campaign to mobilize women voters to support Watanuki. They were confident that as women, they, and not Watanuki or his male staff, knew how to do this best. One of the leaders of the group, the wife of a Takaoka physician, spoke at the women's gathering held in the headquarters' main hall one afternoon. She was cheerful and visibly excited and began her speech with these proud words: "This year is a very busy year for me. It started with a local election, which was followed by the upper house election in the summer. Now, at the year's end, we are in the middle of the general election." Her group decided who should make a campaign speech (Watanuki himself, or his wife, or Watanuki's brother's wife, who lives in Takaoka), where it should be given, and who should be specifically invited to that meeting.

This example may give the impression that such support groups were well organized, had a consistent command system, and made orderly decisions. The reality was rather different. At one corner of the headquarters, a half-dozen women of the group spent several hours discussing over tea and snacks who should have a larger say in deciding who to invite to the campaign meetings—the physician's wife or Watanuki's brother's wife? No conclusion was reached. The talk itself was not a systematic discussion aimed at making a decision. It was, to each participant, more an occasion to express herself generally, that is, her philosophy, her belief, and her values, rather than one to give her particular, concrete opinion on the specific discussion subject. The talk was fragmented, and often a question was not quite answered. Still, without concrete decisions, and, hence without much consistency in a plan, they worked closely later on.

As exemplified in this case, the most significant thing that occurred at the campaign headquarters was that people there (staff, the candidate himself, his family, members of his support groups, and visitors) were expressing their *Selves* to each other in general terms while eating from the same serving plate, drinking from the same kettle, and sharing a heater, table, and floor pillow. The group included even one old man who happened to live near the headquarters but was not a member of any support group. He came to the headquarters every morning. He sat cross-legged beside a heater and enjoyed occasional chatting over tea and food. No one ever tried to keep him out. It is indeed not an exaggeration to say that at the campaign headquarters little discriminatory treatment existed toward anyone, including candidates, based on their socioeconomic statuses, educational backgrounds, sex, or ages.

On one occasion, Watanuki's younger daughter, fresh out of college, accompanied her mother to a small gathering of women voters. Before the speech, a moderator of that meeting introduced Watanuki's daughter to the audience using the honorific term *sama*. The moderator was later criticized for her discriminatory treatment. "Why on earth should she be called sama?" they said. Oda (1982, 67) does not exaggerate when he states that "during an election, the line between the public and private disappears temporarily so that a public figure, that is, politician-candidate and the people of his constituency experience oneness together. That is, the community, the company, and the support groups of the candidate experience a total merger with the candidate as equal human beings."

A twenty-three-year old woman who joined Watanuki's staff for the first time said, "I was surprised at the atmosphere of the headquarters when I came here first, but soon my surprise changed into a deep, emotional involvement. Here, I can feel that each person's power is merged into one so as to create a vast energy. That overwhelms me."[39] At any headquarters, it was not difficult to find de-

[39] Remarks by Senda Akiko, *Toyama Shimbun*, Dec. 9, 1983, p. 3.

voted staff who were willing to stay until midnight or even sleep there overnight.[40]

At first glance, the campaign headquarters may, as described so far, appear to be a Tower of Babel, and in a practical sense, extremely inefficient and wasteful. Nonetheless, this chaotic time and space in a Buddhist temple during the fifteen-day period was a great communitas that created and rejuvenated bonds of whole-human-to-whole-human between people and the candidates. Only with this bond would various support groups be willing to accept and reconfirm candidate-politicians as honorary heads of their groups.

Moreover, this was the occasion in which an entire community was involved in an exciting mock war (Burgess 1986; Haberman 1986). Even the majority of people who neither directly committed themselves to the campaigning nor personally met a candidate were not indifferent. From housewives to elderly people who rarely went out, almost all potential voters were excited and restless. In public, they might complain that candidates A, B, and C annoyed them with phone calls asking for votes. Nonetheless, they would feel alienated and humiliated if only one candidate (not several) called to ask for support. Or, people would be jealous if a candidate called their neighbors or colleagues but ignored them. Any candidate's headquarters knew this point well.[41] Thus, the telephone campaigning was not aimed at explaining the candidate's policies or political stance. Its objective, in one way or another, was to relate each person called to the candidate. A typical conversation, therefore, went like this:

> Hello, is Mr. Nishin Tasuke [full-name] there? I am calling from the campaign headquarters of the Liberal Democratic party candidate, Watanuki Tamisuke. Ms. Yaoya Ohachi [who may be Nishin's friend, or colleague, or relative] kindly introduced you to us. Please, you, too, give Watanuki warm support on the December 18 election day.

That is all that was prepared in advance. After this opening, a conversation might develop about the caller's, Watanuki's, or the recipient's personal relations, children's school, business, and so forth. The same kind of conversation is heard all over the community. On the phone, at the campaign headquarters, at cafeterias, on the streets, at supermarket stores, at work places, and in living rooms, election is the topic of casual conversations. The election, however, is not the political issue. The topic is the voters themselves. Who is on which side? With what connections can one support the particular

[40] Ibid.

[41] Hayakawa Yasuko, one of Watanuki's secretaries, drew my attention to this point.

candidate? Should one take the side of one's union's favorite candidate or the side of another candidate who is one's wife's remote relative? These are examples of the topics people tirelessly and enthusiastically talk about. In some cases, people who happen to support the same candidate build a close relationship with one another. In other cases, a husband and wife find themselves in opposing camps. In so doing, each voter's personal and social networks surface for self-reexamination. Both old and new friends, relatives, acquaintances, and the voters' own states of being in the vast social networks appear before them with new faces, embodying different values and meanings. Voters are provided with opportunities to reflect on their relationships with others and their positions in an entire society while reexamining who they are and how they know they are.

Political issues—even the issue of consumer prices, which public opinion surveys usually show to be the priority concern of the voters—were rarely mentioned. As one of Watanuki's campaign staff, I made at least thirty calls per day in the second half of the campaign period. Only two persons referred to a political issue, namely, political corruption (the Lockheed scandal, which involved former prime minister Tanaka Kakuei and some other senior LDP Diet members as well), although the opposition and the media treated this as a major campaign topic. One was an elderly woman in her seventies, and the other was a middle-aged high school teacher. Both said that they did not like the alleged bribery case of the former prime minister and that they would not personally trust Watanuki because he belonged to the Tanaka faction. It is indicative that what was at issue to both of them was not quite the political corruption at the national level. Instead, their dissatisfaction seemed to derive from their belief that Watanuki betrayed their personal trust by remaining in the faction led by the alleged bribery criminal.

Discussion

Often students of Japanese politics and political culture tend to overlook the significance of this symbolic aspect of an election. That is, an election is an occasion in which personal bonds between the politician-candidate and the people of the constituency are created and recreated and also exposed to become the subject of individual and community self-reexamination. A few scholars, such as Geertz (1972), take this reflexive dimension of human life in seemingly practical occasions seriously. Election campaigning in Japan, like Geertz's

"Deep Play" (that is, betting among the Balinese on cockfights),[42] creates spatially as well as temporally a grand-scale communitas.

The occurrences at the campaign headquarters manifest how the relationship between a politician-candidate and the people of the constituency is and how the former can become "the representative" of the constituency. Winning a certain amount of votes may technically give a candidate a seat in the Diet once, but that will not suffice to make him the representative of the constituency. Nor would strategically organizing various groups of people as potential support bases automatically assure a politician-candidate of loyal support from these people.

Except during the election period, a candidate-politician usually resides in Tokyo and comes back to a constituency, at best, only on weekends. Thus, in an election, the candidate and the people of a constituency are together engaging—in discontinued space and time from the ordinary world—in the construction and reconstruction of their relationship as equal whole-humans. Moreover, the overpowering orgiastic atmosphere during an election, throughout the entire constituency and not just at the campaign headquarters, provides a reflexive occasion in which people have an opportunity to reflect on how they are and how their relationships are with their representatives, so that they can tell their story themselves. This reflexive experience is three-dimensional, involving cosmos, nomos, and chaos, rather than limited to the nomos alone. From the constituents point of view, a candidate-politician, stranger-king, is routinely domesticated and redomesticated at every election time. From the standpoint of candidate-politicians, their statuses as symbolic heads of various associations and private circles and as the representatives of their constituencies, are created and recreated in elections.

If we look at the encounter and merger between a candidate-politician and the people in this way, it is difficult to accept a popular view that regards ordinary people as short-sighted, apathetic individuals who tend to cast their votes because they are given money, promised certain benefits, or told whom to vote for by a local political strongman. Similarly, candidate-politicians should not be identified simplistically as manipulative figures who treat people of their constituencies as if they were their children, that is, maintaining a so-called oyabun-kobun (parent-child) relationship.[43]

[42] See also Ohnuki-Tierney (1984, 208–11).

[43] To view Japanese society in general as consisting of oyabun-kobun relationships at various levels became popular among foreign as well as Japanese scholars, especially since Nakane (1970, especially 40–80, 93–97). Curtis (1971, chap. 2), too, devotes

Seen in the framework of our three-dimensional world, the relationship between the people of the community and a candidate-politician consists of a series of shared moments of liminal experiences. The intrusions of a liminal domain cannot help but dereify the context. Categories of clear, formally differentiated roles and statuses between an elite candidate-politician and the people become invalidated. In such fluid conditions, differentiation between superiors and inferiors would not be possible or meaningful, and there would no longer be an absolute standard of value upon which a cost-benefit or cause-effect calculation would be possible.[44] The orgiastic occurrences during the campaign period, especially those at the campaign headquarters, are seen to be a manifestation of their three-dimensional relationship. An election is a mirror that reflects and makes people activate their reflexivity about how their relationships are and how they know they are. It is also a public bath wherein people are all equally "naked" (dropping their guard) to "see" themselves as well as others and their life-worlds in ways they rarely can while attaining an extraordinary closeness among themselves as equal whole-humans.

---

one chapter to explaining how oyabun-kobun networks and relationships work as a vote-getting machine.

[44] See in this relation, Curtis (1971, 236–42), for his observant statement that money involved in an election campaign is more an expression of gratefulness for support than bribery; also see Representative Fukaya Takashi's lecture before the Liberal Democratic party members at the 1982 party summer seminar for his experience-based conviction that the only important thing is having direct relationships with people based on sincerity rather than on a cost-benefit calculation or a give-and-take transaction (Fukaya 1982, especially 8–15).

Chapter Three

SYMBOLIC INTERLUDES IN POLITICAL LIFE

COMEDIANS, LAUGHTER, AND PLAY

Comedians and Laughter

IN MODERN TIMES comedians have found a new suitable media, television, through which they appeal to an unprecedentedly large audience. Indeed, as McLuhan (1964) so imaginatively argues, television, unlike books, is a great relativizer, a trickster of modern times, which presents to the audience a metaphorically connected (in contrast to metonymically connected, i.e., in a hierarchical, cause-effect relationship) in-the-process reality.

Commenting on the rise of a new kind of comedians in contemporary Japan, Matsuo (1986) ponders that the more or less orthodox type of comedian who works hard to create funny story lines and actions or to master the art of comedy seems to be making an exit. One of the most popular comedians of the new kind is Beat Takeshi, whose extraordinary popularity is such that the term "Takeshi phenomenon" was once widely used. At his peak, Takeshi had five regular television shows and one radio talk show of his own per week besides a few guest appearances (Matsuo, 40–41).

What Takeshi does in these happening-stricken shows is to make any taken-for-granted ideas, values, institutions, and practices of contemporary Japanese life appear to be odd, something to be laughed at by the Japanese people themselves. In his shows, seriousness, hard work, self-sacrifice, and loyalty, for instance, are neither particularly looked up to nor attached to higher moral value. Moreover, his show is often made to lack consistency, organization, or certain intended messages. It also frequently violates lines that separate public and private and reality and illusion by abruptly creating a carnival-like universe, what Takeshi calls an *event*, at an unexpected time and place.

His typical show, such as "Exciting TV with Takeshi the Genius!!" consists of a live studio audience, Takeshi and his company, event reporters, who are half-serious on-site reporters, event moderators, and agitators all at the same time, and who often are part of the event themselves. Four parties, studio audience, Takeshi and company, event reporters, and a large number of the outside audience (sometimes 50,000) of the event develop, as soon as the show starts, a feeling of guilt pleasure, that is, a secret excitement before something outrageous—something that ordinarily remains submerged morally, socially, aesthetically, or factually—is going to happen, and every one of them is not just an onlooker but a willing collaborator of the chief conspirator, Takeshi, who makes it happen.

In one of the "Exciting TV with Takeshi the Genius!!" shows, the event was called "Revitalization Project Goes to a Hot Spring Town." The main target was a desolate local inn in a famous seaside resort town. Upon the arrival of a strange assortment of people and creatures brought by the "Revitalization Project," the town was turned into a "Carnival of Rio" (Beat Takeshi 1986, 148). A carnival procession was, under the cruel summer heat, led by the town's two beauty queens, who were accompanied by a sacred palanquin, Fish-Man (a special half-fish, half-human creature that Takeshi's show invented), a Tahitian dancing troop, a gang of Marilyn Monroe look-alikes, a couple of ponies, and a huge statue of Buddha, whose body almost completely blocked the street. As this gaudy and strange carnival procession moved on toward the inn, the crowd swelled, and a sense of excitement overpowered the area.

Upon arrival, the inn's owner, an old lady in a beautiful kimono, was presented a set of special gifts that had been solemnly carried by the procession. The gifts from Takeshi were a large, fat, gaudily painted porcelain Takeshi-cat hot water fountain to be set in an inn's public bath, a Takeshi-cat clock, and a Takeshi-cat statue, which, sitting at the front door, was thought to have the magic power to attract clients. The gift presentation ritual was led by Takeshi's event reporter, who wore a top hat and cutaway coat and performed on a stage set in front of the inn before the huge, hot crowd who had been following the procession all the way to its destination. And when the statue of Buddha, which was supposed to remain in a metal-cold world of silence, began to utter the "congratulatory speech," the audience, onlookers, and Takeshi's studio audience together burst into thunderous applause. They were one group of active participants in the event, which now became a real thing on its own, occupying special temporal and spatial territory intruded in the interstices of the people's ordinary daily lives.

People were laughing loudly at every part of the onstage performance that dryly mocked and exaggerated what Japanese people usually do. That is, their addiction to gift giving and the empty formality they adhere to in many aspects of Japanese life are used to expose their arbitrariness and contradictiousness. Indeed, as Kundera (1988, 24) contemplates, a comic "reveals the meaninglessness of everything." And this kind of laughter is "directed at all and everyone" (Bakhtin 1984, 11), including those who are laughing around the stage; that is, the "entire world is seen in its droll aspect, in its gay relativity."

As seen in this example of Takeshi's show, the target of the new kind of comedians in contemporary Japan is the abstract—for example, moral, aesthetic, social, and religious—values and beliefs that are deeply rooted in Japan's cultural mold, not concrete people, laws, or policies. Naturally, these comedians take the side of no political group, no ideology, and no social cause. This recent trend in Japan, exemplified in the "Takeshi phenomenon," should be seen as not simply a fad nor peculiar to Japanese society. As Foucault and Marcuse point out, in an industrially advanced society, highly sophisticated information networks and technological marvels have transformed the face of power from that of the premodern repressive king into one that is invisible, neutral, ubiquitous, and often unfelt, or even soothing. In such a postmodern society, skew relativizers of the existing order rather than an organized, serious, outright resistance against state power or authorities can be more effective and better suited to resist domination of a new kind of power.[1] These ubiquitous, shapeless, and evasive deformers, in other words, seem to be truly effective agents that could provide the condition in which the otherwise unseen true nature of such power could be revealed.

Takeshi succinctly shows the essence of contemporary comedians. That is, they expose the arbitrariness of what is taken for granted in the world, including Takeshi and those who are laughing at it, and poke fun at it. They do so not by attacking or criticizing it outright but by revealing in a skewed way the limit, meaninglessness, or inconsistency that is inherent in it. In a word, they relativize absolutely everything. This is what constitutes the basic attitude of Japan's new kind of comedians. Comedians do not appeal to the consciousness of the people nor would they be eager to offer an alternative, consistent worldview in order to denounce or transform the existing order. Their appeal can be received directly through people's intuition and thereby affect their cosmos rather than nomos. The shocks comedians give the audience would lead to the suspension of the flow of ordinary time and help it slip into a spatially, temporary liminal phase where people's reflexivity is activated, as indicated by the fact that comedians in general, and Takeshi in particular, arouse people's ability to feel and sense rather than reason.

---

[1] See in this light, Deleuze and Guattari (1977); Asada (1983, 1986).

Play

As mentioned in chapter 1, some notable scholars have seen the sacred dimension in play. Bataille (1951), Huizinga (1955), Schiller (1965), and Marcuse (1966, 172–96) all agree that in play we experience a departure from the ordinary world and share with others sacred, or liminal moments. Play, as Bataille emphasizes, contradicts all these serious, productive human endeavors. Play, all of them suggest, demands a whole-human's total involvement.[2] In play, people not only discard all nomos constraints including statuses, roles, values, and order so that spontaneous, egalitarian principle overpowers but also, as Geertz (1972) shows in his compelling account, they take the opportunity to activate their reflexivity, that is, to reexamine themselves as well as others and society.

The play element is found universally and ubiquitously, said Huizinga. It is found even at the core of the establishment, as in a faction of Japan's ruling Liberal Democratic party. A minor faction headed by the former LDP vice-president Shiina Etsusaburō, which was dissolved after his death in 1979, enjoyed some quite playful, intimate occasions, owing partly to the small number of its members (between eleven and twenty). One member, former Justice Minister Hamano Seigo described such occasions as "naked" (*hadaka no*) intimacy (Shiina Etsusaburō Tsuitōroku Kankōkai 1982, 51). Beyond just dining and drinking together, the faction members took lessons as a group from a professional teacher in the old Japanese dance *kiyomoto* to the accompaniment of a samisen and a song.

Never in serious competition, their dancing was purely playful. Occasionally, in the evening, they got together to show off their dancing. Each member had at least one specialty in which he parodied an original dance. While dinner was still in progress, the power of sake would seduce a member into advancing to the front of a tatami floor to present his dance. Members competed for neither techniques nor mastery. Instead, they devoted themselves only to appearing laughingly foolish, nonsensical, and hilarious. Seriousness was completely out of place in their dancing. For example, the pictures show Shiina dancing his original number entitled, *Noguso odori* (dance of dropping feces in the field), exposing his thighs and walking like a duck. Others were as hilariously nonsensical as Shiina's, including *Daruma odori* (dance of a tumbler), *Tankō odori* (a coal mi-

---

[2] On this crucial point, Caillois (1959, 152–62; Caillois 1961) is a dissident who asserts that to people the play world is a carefree land whose only constraints are play rules.

ner's dance), and *Hanakuso odori* (nose-picking dance) (Shiina 1982, 50).

Vulgar words that ordinarily were seldom mentioned, like *noguso* (feces dropped outside) and *hanakuso* (nose dirt), were especially favored in their dancing. Shamelessness like showing thighs, imitating a tumbler, picking the nose exaggeratedly, and performing the relief of nature on the fringe of someone else's garden were supremely praiseworthy. Taboos of nomos were joyfully breached. Politeness, seriousness, order, and the moral code had no meaning or value here. Vulgarity, absurdity, nonsense, spontaneity, and immediacy overpowered this play world of the usually serious and pretentious Japanese Diet members. Play turned the politicians into a gang of fools. Fools experienced a fools' world that existed in symbolic time and space, not within the domain of nomos.[3] As mentioned, members felt in these occasions a "naked" intimacy. This is exactly what V. Turner called whole-human-to-whole-human bonds.

These were the occasions for self-reexamination, as was the Balinese cockfight, which Geertz (1972) called "Deep Play." Experiences of a symbolic fools' world in play may well have the potential to provide the members with opportunities to bend on themselves. Furthermore, intrusions of such liminal states of play bring in ambiguities and inconsistencies so that differentiations and boundaries of roles and statuses among the members can blur and formal principles and moral codes appear to be no more than arbitrary. Play, a deformer, thus allows for the condition in which genuine three-dimensional change is possible over time.

SHEDDING TEARS: SUSPENSION OF POLITICS

Even tears can have a potential to suspend politics that is as significant as that of carefully crafted persuasion tactics. This case centers on Nakasone Yasuhiro, prime minister of Japan between 1982 and 1987. It suggests that a whole-human's lifeworld does not constitute a seamless flow of events in sequence or a causal chain, or to put it differently, not in the way that each level is laid one by one in a hierarchy. Quite casually in daily life, a catastrophe or disruption of a causal chain of events takes place because deformative liminal states intrude and overpower. As a consequence, an entire context can be constantly liable to fundamental change. (We will consider this point

---

[3] Welsford (1935); Huizinga (1952); Erasmus (1965); Willeford (1969); Yamaguchi (1969); and Seymour-Ure (1974).

more fully in the concluding chapter.) We may, therefore, need to understand the development of events neither as a linear causal chain nor a pyramid. Instead, we can grasp it more appropriately by conceptualizing its process as consisting of numerous mutually unrelated, qualitatively disparate, or even mutually contradictory phases. It is notable in this connection that recently a few scholars of history and sociology have become interested in applying a theory of catastrophe, as advanced by René Thom (1975), to their respective studies.[4] I will show that politically irrelevant tears could bring about a catastrophe in the political process whereby the subsequent course of events could acquire not only a totally new direction but also a redefinition of the whole context.

Nakasone Yasuhiro was appointed prime minister in November 1982 thanks to the substantial backing of Tanaka Kakuei, the former prime minister from 1972 to 1974. The selection of the ruling Liberal Democratic party president—who will automatically become prime minister because of the LDP's numerical dominance in the Diet—depends heavily on a factional alliance. That is, one who succeeds in forming a factional alliance with one or more of the LDP's five major factions could have a better chance of becoming a party president/ prime minister. When Nakasone was competing in the party presidential race in 1982, his own faction, with its 49 members, was the second smallest among five factions, whereas Tanaka was the head of a gigantic 108-member faction.[5] That without Tanaka's help, Nakasone could not have won the post was no secret to the public. Indeed, his cabinet, which consisted of six members of the Tanaka faction out of twenty ministers was popularly called "Tanakasone" (Tanaka plus Nakasone, meaning Nakasone cabinet under the control of Tanaka). Relying substantially on the numerical strength of the Tanaka faction, however, was to Nakasone not as ominous as the fact that Tanaka was arrested in July 1976 for his involvement in the Lockheed bribery case, and the trial was still in progress. Tanaka kept his Diet seat throughout the period.

It took more than seven years for the Tokyo Local Court to hand down the decision at the first trial. During those seven years of court examinations, it became more and more certain that Tanaka would not be able to win the case. In the concluding statement at the Tokyo Local Court on January 26, 1983, prosecutors proposed for Tanaka a

---

[4] See Noguchi (1973); Aoi (1974, 239–308), Sawa and Ushiki (1975); and Thompson (1979), for example.

[5] Nihon Seikei Shimbunsha, Feb. 1983, 334–37.

five year prison term plus a 500 million yen penalty (approximately $1 = 234 yen at that time).

Given this proposal, the once fading Lockheed issue came to the surface again. Within two weeks, all opposition parties united to propose a draft resolution to the Diet to "recommend" (*kankoku*) Tanaka Kakuei's resignation as a Diet member. The Nakasone government found itself in the center of an extremely difficult and frustrating situation. In particular, Nakasone was almost totally stalemated. If the government allowed the united opposition draft resolution to be approved by the Diet, Tanaka might well be morally and politically forced to resign even though the resolution was not legally binding. His resignation would mean the total collapse of Nakasone's power because (1) withdrawal of all the Tanaka faction's support would reduce Nakasone to little more than the head of a fourth-place faction; and (2) Diet approval of the resolution would mean an acknowledgment of Tanaka's guilt by the government. That, in turn, would mean that the government would admit that it had exercised power with substantial help from the man who was guilty or who, at least, had done something morally and terribly wrong.

Nakasone's dilemma was that he could neither afford to let the resolution receive approval nor reject it outright. If Nakasone prevented the resolution overtly, the media, the public, the opposition, and the nonmainstream LDP factions would severely criticize him for protecting a morally and legally unacceptable man. What can be said of Nakasone in connection with Tanaka's Lockheed bribery case is, however, if to a somewhat lesser degree, also applicable to the LDP at large vis-à-vis the opposition parties and the media (which usually claimed to be reflecting the voices of the general public). Thus, the government had no choice but to delay the Diet approval of the resolution. At the time, in January 1983, the actual number of lower house seats was 499—officially, lower house seats must number 511, but there were twelve vacancies then—and the LDP retained 285, 35 seats more than needed to kill the resolution.

Opposition parties regarded the situation as a golden opportunity to break the LDP majority. They thought that if a general election were held in the middle of the period in which the Tanaka issue dominated the public, they could "win big." Here, we see a twist of interest on the part of the opposition parties. That is, even though they overtly requested an immediate resignation of Tanaka and pushed the resolution hard to get Diet approval, if Tanaka really had resigned from the Diet, they would have lost their major weapon and, hence, missed the opportunity to break the LDP majority rule. In other words, it was in their true interest for Tanaka stubbornly to remain a Diet member.

With interests on both sides concurring, at the end of the 98th ordinary Diet in May, the government decided to carry over the resolution to the next Diet session. The LDP could avoid overtly rejecting the resolution, whereas the opposition found it advantageous to appear to the public as the determined pursuer of justice for a longer period of time. The 99th extraordinary Diet, which followed the 13th House of Councilors' election on June 26 for formality's sake, lasted for only six days without any substantial discussion. Actually, therefore, the resolution was shelved until the 100th extraordinary Diet session in September. Meanwhile, the news spread in late June that the Tokyo Local Court would hand down the decision on the Tanaka case at the first trial on October 12. The public and the media now saw the 100th Diet as a battlefield for decisive fights between the opposition and the ruling LDP in connection with the case, and at the same time, between Nakasone and nonmainstream factions within the LDP. Besides, how Nakasone would manage to escape from the stalemate became the favorite topic of discussion in almost the entire mass media by early September. Such major journals as *Asahi Jānaru*, *Ekonomisuto*, *Chūō Kōron*, and *Bungei Shunjū* devoted considerable space throughout 1983 to articles—many of them special features—on the Tanaka-Nakasone Lockheed issue.

In late summer 1983, mainstream factions—that is, factions that together constituted a majority to effect the favorable allocation of cabinet as well as Diet posts—of Tanaka, Suzuki, and Nakasone indicated their preference for preventing the opposition-proposed pending resolution from reaching the Diet main floor. Nonmainstream factions, Fukuda and Kōmoto, on the other hand, kept their positions ambiguous by arguing that without being sure what the October 12 court decision could be, it was unwise to speak much about it.

More voices were heard among the younger members of the Fukuda, Kōmoto, and Suzuki factions. They maintained that if the resolution reached the Diet for a vote, they would abstain so that the opposition's votes would constitute a majority. These younger Diet members had not yet built strong support bases in their constituencies in Japan's harshly competitive multicandidate electoral district system. With a strong possibility that the general election might be held after the court decision, they were eager not to appear as to be allies or supporters of Tanaka to the voters. They feared that the Tanaka case could have a devastating effect on their election. This desire to keep a distance and difference between themselves and Tanaka was, more or less, overtly or covertly, shared among the LDP Diet members, including Nakasone. According to the *Mainichi Shimbun* opinion survey conducted in September among the LDP Diet members, three-fourths of the members of mainstream factions such as Nakasone's and Suzuki's responded with the opinion that Tanaka should resign from the Diet if he was found guilty. In the Tanaka faction, less than a majority of the members (38 percent) supported Tanaka's resignation, whereas the rest of the Tanaka faction said that he need not resign ("Jimintōnai ni takamaru," 1983, 7).

To Tanaka Kakuei, unlike most LDP members, the earliest possible general election was the most desirable. He was confident that even if an election were held in the wake of the negative court decision, he and his faction could win.[6] Tanaka had been frantically pursuing a numerical expansion of his faction as well as strengthening every member's electoral basis in preparation for the worst court decision. Since his arrest in 1976 the number of his faction members had steadily increased. To keep a larger number of strong members was certainly a clever strategy for effectively coping with possible hardships brought on during the long court struggle.[7] With sure conviction, what Tanaka wanted most was to "purify" (*misogi*) his guilt[8] by undergoing public judgment, that is, by running for a general election as soon as possible.

The opposition, too, wanted an election immediately after the court decision. They had already agreed that they would force the government to hold the earliest possible election if the October 12 court decision found Tanaka guilty. In the opposition's view, the fresher, the more salient, and the more dominant the Tanaka bribery issue was, the better chance they would have to win the election. Nakasone may have been more afraid of election defeat than were any younger LDP Diet members. He wanted to go on to the second two-year term of the party presidency. His first term was to expire in November 1984. To be reelected as president, an impressive election

[6] See for example, his comments on October 13 to the effect that what really mattered to the constituency was the undramatic daily efforts politicians have made for and with people rather than distant events at the national level (Asahi Shimbun Seijibu, 1985, 120). And he was proved right in the December 1983 general election. Not only did he himself win the largest number of votes, 220,761, in Japan's postwar electoral history but his faction also survived well (Nihon Seikei Shimbunsha, Feb. 1984, 294–306, 334–36).

[7] For the Tanaka faction's expansion strategy in connection to the Lockheed scandal case, see Asahi Shimbun Seijibu (1985, 144–50) and Matsumoto (1983).

[8] For purification of guilt, an indigenous concept of Japan traced back to mythology, see Ohnuki-Tierney (1984, chap. 2). In modern times, too, the same concept has been applied to a number of political corruption cases, see Murobushi (1981).

victory for the party would help greatly. When a party loses badly, Japan's party head is supposed to resign to take responsibility for that failure. This is true not only of the conservative ruling LDP but also of the opposition parties. Thus, Nakasone's presidency was at stake in the general election. Naturally, he wanted to avoid any negative factors that would lead to the LDP's election defeat. At the same time, however, he had to keep in mind that the loss of Tanaka's support for him meant his (Nakasone's) fall.

With the opening of the Diet session on September 8, 1983, all opposition parties tried hard to revive the pending resolution. In response, the government raised a counter argument to the effect that guilty verdicts at the first instance should not mean that the persons are guilty because they can appeal to the higher courts; and that to ostracize the Diet member whose guilt is not yet finally decided by the judicature is an abuse of legislative power and, hence, is against the basic principle of separation of powers.[9]

On October 12, Tokyo's all six television stations focused on the court decision for Tanaka's bribery case. A total of forty hours was devoted to Tanaka-related programs from early morning ("Sonohi no Tanaka," 1983, 12–15). At around ten o'clock, the Tokyo Local Court ruled that the former prime minister was guilty and sentenced him to four years of prison and a fine of 500 million yen. Immediately after the verdict, Tanaka filed an appeal to the higher court.[10] Although the decision as such was widely expected, the shock it caused was really serious; continuation of the Diet session seemed inconceivable. The prospect of resolving the tension was shattered when Tanaka, upon returning home after having paid the bail of 200 million yen, released a statement saying that he greatly regretted the court decision and that to prove his innocence he would fight as long as he lived. The tone of the statement was surprisingly aggressive; even those who had seen a slight possibility of Tanaka's resignation until that morning instantly realized that Tanaka had absolutely no intention of resigning voluntarily.

Opposition parties moved swiftly. As early as eleven o'clock, the secretary-general of the Kōmeitō, the middle-of-the-road party, stood on one of Tokyo's busiest streets urging passers-by at the top of his voice to judge as voters whether Tanaka ought to be made to resign. Another middle-of-the-road party, the Democratic Socialist party (DSP) had already started a marathon speech session the previous

[9] On this point, see Asahi Jānaru Henshūbu (1983a).

[10] By law, he can appeal to two more courts; the Tokyo High Court and the Supreme Court.

night at another busy spot in the town. The Japan Socialist party (JSP) and its major support body, the General Council of Japan Labor Unions, went to a demonstration on the busy Tokyo street with a huge banner, the width of ten persons, that read, "Tanaka Kakuei, Resign from the Diet, Immediately!" Inside the Diet, the opposition decided that they would boycott all Diet sessions unless the government immediately put the pending resolution to a discussion.

Members attending the October 14 LDP Executive Board meeting were told by the party's Diet Policy Committee chairman and the Nakasone faction member, Okonogi Hikosaburō, that the constitutionality of the resolution that "recommended" Tanaka's resignation was questionable. He referred here to the principle of separation for the three powers. Therefore, he went on to argue, the LDP should not allow it to reach the Diet. The executive board acknowledged that position. Nonetheless, a sign of intraparty rift emerged from that meeting. The nonmainstream Kōmoto faction and others later strongly protested by arguing that to acknowledge someone's opinion was one thing but to support it was another. The rather strong distaste of nonmainstream factions, especially of the Kōmoto faction, for the Nakasone government's protective attitude toward Tanaka is revealed in the *Asahi Shimbun* opinion survey among all 286 LDP lower house Diet members shortly after the October 12 court decision. Asked whether Tanaka should completely withdraw from the Diet—that is, not just resign but whether he should be banned totally from future participation in the Diet—69.0 percent of the Kōmoto faction said yes (table 3.1). The data also disclose other factions' distance and the conflict and/or congruence of interests with the Tanaka fac-

TABLE 3.1
Opinion Survey among the Members of the LDP Factions on Tanaka's Resignation: Should the Former Prime Minister, Tanaka, Leave the Political World Entirely? (N = 242)

Factions	Yes	(%)	Let Him Decide by Himself	(%)	Unnecessary	(%)	Other	(%)
Nakasone	6	14.3	17	40.5	13	31.0	6	14.3
Tanaka	0	0.0	12	22.6	41	77.4	0	0.0
Suzuki	16	29.6	22	40.7	6	11.1	10	18.5
Fukuda	17	47.2	9	25.0	2	5.6	8	22.2
Kōmoto	20	69.0	3	10.3	2	6.9	4	13.8
Independents	1	3.6	17	60.7	3	10.7	7	25.0

Source: Asahi Shimbun Seijibu (1985, 115–17).

tion. Tanaka's own faction aside, the Nakasone faction was the most reluctant to ostracize Tanaka from the Diet.

In contrast, the concern of members of the nonmainstream Fukuda and Kōmoto factions apparently was how to dissociate themselves from Tanaka in the eyes of the general public while not disenchanting voters with the LDP as a whole. Thus, 72.2 percent of the Fukuda faction and 79.3 percent of the Kōmoto faction seemed to prefer a Tanaka-as-scapegoat strategy. The long-time fraternal relationship of the Suzuki faction with the Tanaka faction seemed to prevent it from launching a direct and explicit challenge to Tanaka, even though a majority of its members secretly hoped for Tanaka's retirement. The largest portion of the Suzuki faction, thus, liked a softer, indirect attitude.

Nakasone was stalemated by the slight possibility of Tanaka's voluntary resignation, the unusually tough stance of the opposition, which was backed by the media and the public, and the pressure from within his own party. He could not be sure whether the nonmainstream factions would cooperate with him. Even worse was the possibility that portions of the nonmainstream Fukuda and Kōmoto factions might either abstain or vote for the resolution if it actually came up for a vote. Moreover, a delaying tactic was not available this time. Tanaka, the opposition, and nonmainstream factions saw a swift move as their advantage, as we have seen. In the meantime, the Diet had already halted. The media's focus on the Tanaka issue did not seem to be fading. The longer a period like this lasted, the more critical the public would become of the LDP. Nakasone was under heavy pressure to take immediate action.

While the Diet halted for about ten days, the LDP's nonmainstream factions started moving as they sensed a shift of the general mood of Nagatachō. By then, that Tanaka should be asked to resign had become the subject of popular talks among politicians. A senior official of the nonmainstream Fukuda faction noted on October 21 that the issue now was how Tanaka could be made to resign, not whether he should resign, and that without Tanaka's resignation, no breakthrough was possible. On the same day, former Prime Minister Miki Takeo—Tanaka was arrested in 1976 while Miki was the prime minister—visited the official residence of Nakasone to urge that Tanaka be asked to resign. Miki, who had been replaced by Kōmoto Toshio as the faction head, still held enough authority on party affairs to make people listen to him. A Fukuda faction high-ranking official immediately expressed his support for Miki's action. Moreover, Miki talked with the opposition party leaders the next day on the Tanaka issue. The Tanaka side was not defeated by these new moves. The monthly newsletter of his support organization, *Gekkan Etsuzan*, which was issued on October 24, carried a large headline on the front page that insisted that Tanaka and his supporters would only move forward and never withdraw one inch.

Nakasone had been trying desperately through an intermediary to persuade Tanaka to resign. He had spoken with various persons whom Tanaka would listen to and who were willing to play go-between. These emissaries included certain influential retired politicians, senior officials in both the Tanaka and Nakasone factions, and party executives (Sasaki 1983a). Two weeks of exhaustive efforts, however, were futile. Tanaka's determination could not be shaken. As a last resort, the LDP officials started considering two measures: (1) Nikaidō Susumu, the Tanaka faction's nominal head and the LDP secretary-general, would be sent to Tanaka to inform him of Nakasone's "determination to dissolve the Diet" and to present him with "the election timetable." In exchange, Nikaidō would advise Tanaka to resign from the Diet and come back soon by winning the scheduled election; (2) the LDP would deliberately let the resolution reach the Diet for a vote. Then, they would bargain with Tanaka by telling him that if he accepted resignation, the resolution could be killed by the LDP's majority votes.

In the meantime, the LDP's top executives had been considering for a few days whether to send a letter from Nakasone to Tanaka to seek any possible compromise from him to break an ever-stiffening political impasse. On October 26, the party executives met with Nakasone, advocating that he write a letter to Tanaka. Nakasone told them, "By its nature, a letter cannot help being formal and consisting of more reasons than warm human emotions. As his long-time friend, I myself will meet him face-to-face to talk in heartfelt words" (Sasaki 1983b, 20). Some top executives of the party opposed the idea of a one-on-one meeting with Tanaka; Nakasone insisted, however. Still, it took a day for the party executives finally to agree to a Nakasone-Tanaka direct meeting plan. To Nakasone and to the rest as well, nothing was guaranteed. Given the fact that Tanaka agreed to meet Nakasone face-to-face only after Tanaka's two most trusted LDP seniors, Secretary-General Nikaidō Susumu and Chief Cabinet Secretary Gotōda Masaharu had patiently persuaded him, even a most optimistic person felt that there might be at best a fifty-fifty chance for Tanaka's resignation (Sasaki 1983b, 21).

Because Nakasone wanted to talk to Tanaka with emotion (*jō*) rather than reason (*ri*), the place was set in a homey hotel suite that consisted of a twin bedroom and a cozily furnished living room. According to the most reliable accounts presented by the *Asahi Shimbun* political section (Asahi Shimbun Seijibu 1985, 121–29) and other reports that appeared in major newspapers and journals at that time, at around afternoon tea time, Tanaka and Nakasone started to chat over tea, melon, and cake. As soon as they were left alone behind closed doors, Nakasone first called Tanaka by the amicable nickname, "Kaku-*san*" with a break in his voice. Tanaka, in response, said, "I regret causing you a lot of trouble," adding, "Thank you very much for sending me flowers the other day" (referring to his illness in early October).

The one hour and forty minute private meeting contained no mention of Tanaka's resignation. They reminisced about their early days as passionate and naive young politicians in the chaotic era that followed immediately after Japan's war defeat. Nakasone then expressed his heartfelt sympathy to Tanaka in connection with the Lockheed scandal by noting that he was the one who understood most how Tanaka felt about it because he, too, was once summoned to testify at the lower house special committee for the Lockheed case investigation during the height of the scandal in 1977.[11] He related quietly, "I, too, was under intensive, harsh attacks then. My family could not help crying in those circumstances" (Asahi Shimbun Seijibu 1985, 124). Nakasone suggested that Tanaka be prudent in going through the current difficult situation and made a friendly comment that Tanaka's statement right after the court decision on October 12 sounded a little too aggressive. Tanaka agreed and promised Nakasone that he would be very prudent henceforth.

After the talk over tea, each of them issued a statement. Nakasone noted:

> I had a talk with Tanaka Kakuei-*kun* [*kun* is a much friendlier way to speak of a person than the ordinary *san*, or *shi* and is usually used among very close friends, such as classmates and golfing buddies] as a friend of his about various current problems. . . .
>
> Tanaka-kun and I were both first elected in 1947 and since then for some thirty-six years we have made efforts together to rebuild our country while always sharing warm friendship. . . .
>
> Tanaka-kun is now facing an extremely difficult situation. I know too well how Tanaka-kun and his family feel about it. I cannot help having compassion for them. . . .
>
> As a friend of his I provided him with advice as much as I could." (Asahi Shimbun Seijibu 1985, 126–27)

---

[11] Because Nakasone was the minister of International Trade and Industry when the Tanaka cabinet made the decision to purchase Lockheed airbuses, his involvement in the bribery case was investigated then.

Meanwhile, Tanaka issued a brief statement to show his gratitude to Nakasone for his consideration. In a longer statement issued three days later, Tanaka expressed deep regret at having caused trouble to the people, especially to the members of the Liberal Democratic party. The tone of the statement showed a remarkable contrast with the first one issued right after the court decision some twenty days before. The second statement sounded humble, modest, and low-postured (Asahi Shimbun Seijibu 1985, 127–29).

It was too optimistic to think that the Tanaka-Nakasone face-to-face meeting and the issuance of the significantly softened Tanaka statement that followed could satisfy nonmainstream factions of the LDP as well as opposition parties. The opposition flatly regarded the meeting as a ritual to prepare for forcefully normalizing the Diet. The nonmainstream factions demanded that Nakasone disclose exactly what he had told Tanaka and what Tanaka's responses were. The LDP's thirty-member executive board held an informal gathering the morning after Tanaka issued his second statement. The executive board members invited Nakasone to speak directly to them about the Tanaka-Nakasone talk and his intention to cope with the problem.

Before taking a closer look at the executive board informal gathering, it is useful to know how the board is constituted. The Executive Board is by no means dominated by either the Tanaka or Nakasone faction (tables 3.2, 3.3). On the contrary, it is the nonmainstream Fukuda faction that holds both chairman and vice-chairman posts. The Tanaka faction, which is largest in number, maintains fewer seats than the Suzuki or Fukuda faction. Furthermore, the Tanaka faction retains no vice-chairman post for its representatives, although all four other factions send one representative member to that post. In short, in terms of the factional proportion and under those circumstances, the executive board could not be expected to act favorably for Tanaka and Nakasone.

As the breakdown in political age in table 3.3 suggests, all three generations hold a fairly equal proportion of seats. In sharp contrast to Nakasone's and Tanaka's political age, fourteen—that is, both had survived fourteen elections since 1947—the core of the executive board consisted of those middle-echelon members who had been elected from five to seven times and four-term juniors plus eight-term seniors. If a generation gap in terms of political age (not biological age) existed, therefore, it would only adversely affect Nakasone and Tanaka. As a matter of fact, it did exist. According to the previously cited *Asahi Shimbun* opinion survey among all LDP Diet members, the younger the member was, the more he or she tended to be critical of Tanaka (Asahi Shimbun Seijibu 1985, 117). All in all, few

TABLE 3.2
LDP Executive Board Factional Breakdown

Factions	Representatives (Lower House)	Councilors (Upper House)	Total
Mainstream			
Tanaka	4	2[a]	6
Nakasone	2[a]	0	2
Suzuki	7[a]	2	9
Nonmainstream			
Fukuda	4[ab]	3	7
Kōmoto	3[a]	0	3
Independents	2	1	3
Total	22	8	30

Source: Nihon Seikei Shimbunsha (Feb. 1983, vol. 67).
[a] Vice-chairman 1.
[b] Chairman 1.

elements existed in the executive board that Nakasone could effectively exploit to turn the tide.

To everyone's surprise, however, the tide did change. Things started moving again clearly after the executive board meeting. Here, once again, emotion (jō) overpowered reason (ri). Nakasone told the executive board what he and Tanaka had talked about. While he was relating that Tanaka and his family were having an extremely hard time and that he could not help being touched with compassion, Nakasone broke into tears. He pulled out a handkerchief to wipe his eyes. He continued with an effort to say that because he himself was once criticized and doubted in connection with the Lockheed scandal, he could feel a special sympathy with Tanaka. What was needed most, said Nakasone with a break in his voice, was to cry as well as to laugh with Tanaka beside him. Through the end of his more than half-hour talk, Nakasone needed a handkerchief. Nakasone's tears appeared so sincere and pure that not only was an entire room silent with sympathy but a couple of board members also had tears in their eyes.

According to the excerpt of the talk disclosed in the evening issue of major newspapers that day, even the chairman of the executive board, who as a senior member of the nonmainstream Fukuda faction was expected to play a tough prosecutor's role against Nakasone, said that no one could deny that Nakasone's heartfelt talk impressed the executive board. A vice-chairman and senior member of the Fukuda faction also admitted that he was moved. Other non-

TABLE 3.3
LDP Executive Board Political Age Breakdown

Generation	Number of times Elected[a]	Representatives
	14	1
Senior	11	1
	10	1
	8	4[bc]
Total		7
	7	4[c]
Middle-echelon	6	4[d]
	5	1
Total		9
	4	4
Junior	3	1
	2	1
Total		6
Total (all levels)		22

		Councilors
	6	1[c]
	4	2
	3	4
	1	1
Total		8

Source: Nihon Seikei Shimbunsha (Feb. 1983, 67: 85–157, 176, 334–37).
[a] Political age = number of times elected.
[b] Chairman 1.
[c] Vice-chairman 1.
[d] Vice-chairman 2.

mainstream faction members were no exception. The Kōmoto faction members expressed sympathy with Nakasone. The expected harsh accusations that Nakasone should have unambiguously told Tanaka to resign were not heard at the meeting. Although it was suggested by several mainstream as well as nonmainstream faction members that the general public might want to see a clear-cut end to the Tanaka affair—and, therefore, that Nakasone should have taken a decisive stance toward Tanaka—the suggestions were without teeth. When Nakasone was about to leave the room, the board members gave him their hearty applause. After Nakasone left, the executive board's informal gathering was switched to a formal meeting. The members then decided that the Tanaka affair had been tackled hard enough and that now the decision was in Tanaka's hands. That is, the LDP formally decided that the issue ceased to be a party affair.[12]

The media, as usual, was critical of the way the Tanaka affair was shelved. Nonetheless, their general reaction was no more than a half-hearted sarcasm, as exemplified by the *Ekonomisuto* comment, "We Japanese are by nature soft on tears, aren't we? Tears had the issue swept away without really solving it at all" ("Dasan to 'kejime' " 1983, 34). More significantly, though they were critical of the way the issue was ended, few seemed to feel seriously offended by Nakasone's tears. One of the country's three major newspapers, the *Mainichi Shimbun*, carried a column written by its veteran political editor, entitled, "Politicians and Tears." He noted that a politician ought to act with reasons and never expect to escape from his public duties and obligations by capitalizing on people's emotions. However, he went on, he would rather not have those kinds of politicians who are not moved by emotion nor shed tears (Nakada 1983).

Whether with sympathy, sarcasm, or anger, the common denominator of the general reaction to the event was the acknowledgment, if reluctant, that there are ways to get things done outside of the domain of reasons, calculations, material and nonmaterial resources, and the legal system. Until the October 28 Nakasone-Tanaka private meeting, all sides were straightforwardly attempting to cope with the situation within the domain of nomos. Numbers, strategies, calculations, and the legal status were predominantly referred to by every actor. Consequently, they, the actors in opposition to whole-humans, found themselves stuck together in the institutional arrangements of nomos. The more each side tried to rely on nomos measures to break the stalemate, the harder it became. All means in nomos were exhausted.

Discussion

In such an extraordinary stalemate, what Nakasone's tears did was to counterpose incompatible ways of looking at the entire situation. Nakasone's tears helped bring inconsistencies into the context, just like the little boy in the fable who flatly said that the emperor was

[12] Articles are numerous on the LDP Executive Board informal gathering and Nakasone's tears. To list only a few:"Tanaka jishoku 'Jō de unagashita,' " *Yomiuri Shimbun*, Nov. 1, 1983, evening edition, p. 1; "Sokuin no jō, shushō naku (Prime minister was weeping out of sympathy and compassion), *Yomiuri Shimbun*, Nov. 1, 1983, evening edition; for excerpts of the gathering, see ibid., p. 2; " 'Nakisone-san' namida no isseki," *Mainichi Shimbun*, Nov. 1 1983, evening edition; Asahi Jānaru Henshūbu (1983b); and Asahi Shimbun Seijibu (1985, 129–33).

naked; or the popular riddle, "Who is that guy with only one leg and one eye?" "It's a needle"; or the joke, "Can you tell the nationality of that busy shoe black?" Person 1, "Looks Polish" and Person 2, "And never Finnish." That is, by recalling our metonymy-metaphor comparison in chapter 1, we can immediately understand that what Nakasone's tears did was functionally identical with what was brought about by the child, riddle, or joke just cited. By reorganizing elements under a metaphoric principle rather than a linear, irreversible, and hierarchical principle of metonymy, they commonly succeed in deforming the context and, hence, making the existing arrangements of nomos appear no more than arbitrary.

Nakasone's tears aroused a previously unknown, politically irrelevant, and contradictory picture of Tanaka Kakuei as Nakasone's dear friend with whom he shared thirty-six years' experience through the colorful and stormy days of postwar Japan. The Japanese audience was also reminded of the hardship unfairly placed on a defendant's or even a suspect's family. Nakasone's totally unexpected tears of deep sympathy and compassion carried an entire informal gathering away from the nomos domain and threw it altogether into the liminal state. As Leach (1967) cogently argues, such symbolism of hair, tears, or blood is public property—that is, whose immediate source is not private psychology but a cultural rule—and is often considered to *do* things, that is, to alter the situation in a mystical, rather than in a material, sense. In the liminal state, as we have seen in the introductory chapter of Terrence Turner's (1977) theoretical analysis, two mutually incompatible sets of elements were merged into one. Tanaka, Nakasone, and the whole affair now appear to have two mutually contradictory faces; the entire affair can be looked at in two totally different ways as a result of the introduction of new elements invoked by Nakasone's tears. Consequently, the Diet members, media, and the public became free from any set of elements of nomos for a while in the liminal state. And free reorganization of any of these elements is made possible. To them Tanaka came to be seen not as a morally and legally questionable Diet member nor as an attractive, hardworking, warm-hearted, and extraordinarily successful man. Nakasone, likewise, came to appear not as a weak premier who was under pressure to ostracize his crucial patron nor as Tanaka's equal, compassionate friend. Similarly, the entire situation became neither a political stalemate whose breakthrough was possible only by the ostracization of moral and legal evil, Tanaka, nor an ordeal of Tanaka and his family. And the once absolute priority—that is, how the LDP should expel Tanaka from the Diet—appeared to have lost its importance. In the people's perception, definitions and categories of roles, statuses, values, principles, and other institutional arrangements lost their clarity.

Intrusions of these inconsistencies and ambiguities invoked by Nakasone's tears helped deform the context. As a consequence, participants faced blurred boundaries among categories of people, things, and principles. Once articulate and taken-for-granted values, meanings, and definitions no longer appeared to carry exclusive legitimacy or sufficient clarity. Owing to this deformative function of liminal states, people in such situations are provided with an opportunity to see the possibilities of new arrangements of elements. Such new arrangements may include those kinds that are fundamentally destructive to the existing order, as in the case of Nakasone's tears, in which the political and social institutions of nomos were relativized and failed to exercise their legitimate functions in dealing with the redefined situation.

Chapter Four

ON LIMINAL QUALITIES

I N THE INTRODUCTORY CHAPTER, I referred to a trickster as one of the most vivid and universal embodiments of liminality. In addition to some delightfully colorful ethnographic studies of the trickster in various parts of the world from the time of mythology to the modern era,[1] even a psychological study is tried (Jung 1969). When anthropologists were drawn to the uniquely enchanting nature of marginal beings, the trickster appeared as one of its representative embodiments. Many notable anthropologists, therefore, have written about the trickster.[2]

Like any other figure who embodies liminal qualities, tricksters can be found in the interstices, on the margins, or on the bottom of social structure, as V. Turner (1977) suggests. Douglas (1966) sees tricksters along with marginal or peripheral beings as "dirt," that is, matter out of place. Lévi-Strauss (1963) and Leach (1961a) are attracted by trickster figures because of their intermediary roles and mobility, that is, their freedom from any classification: they may belong to two or more mutually incompatible categories at the same time, or they may belong to none. Babcock-Abrahams (1975, 159–60) sums up major characteristics of trickster figures. These characteristics can be applied to marginal beings in general. They include: creative/destructive dualism, multiple identities or none, extraordinary libido, aggressiveness, amorality, and defiance of authority and order. Situated ambiguously in the interstices or at the margins of nomos, or clinging to the bottom of it, they violate social, cultural, spatial, and temporal boundaries by forcefully introducing incompatible elements of other domains. They therefore inevitably blur distinctions between, for example, good and evil and reality and illusion. In short, they are potential deformers of the context.

As Babcock-Abrahams (1975) suggests, through defiance of the existing order, or morality, and of authority in a number of ways, the trickster helps ordinary people have an opportunity to activate and reactivate their reflexivity. Ordinary people, in turn, become aware that anything existing in nomos can be arbitrary and subject to

[1] Wescott (1962); Cox (1969); Radin (1969); and Yamaguchi (1974).

[2] Leach (1961a); Lévi-Strauss (1963); Douglas (1966); V. Turner (1968, 580–81); Yamaguchi (1974, 1977a); and Babcock-Abrahams (1975).

change. Handelman and Kapferer's (1980, 42) term for this function of tricksters in particular and marginal beings and liminal states in general is *deformation* of the existing context. They cannot transform context; but by deforming it, they may function as agents of transformation.

Liminality is a relative concept. Marginal beings and liminal states should not be fixed in a residual category, as Babcock-Abrahams (1975, 155) points out in her criticism of Douglas's later work. Indeed, a review of the literature throughout this book indicates that any person may experience becoming a marginal being or entering liminal states under certain circumstances and that liminality can be embodied by any person, matter, or principle, including even those situated at the center of nomos institutions.

One of my chief objectives in this book is to try to explain power in terms of ordinary people's reflexivity. Naturally, our interest as political scientists is not to find "real" tricksters that appear in mythologies and legends or exist in some isolated indigenous community. We look instead for an embodiment of liminal qualities in people in modern political life. And we do find liminal qualities even in those politicians who are situated at the center of nomos. As the most interesting examples of such politicians in Japan, Nakagawa Ichirō, Tanaka Kakuei, and Nakasone Yasuhiro will be introduced in the following pages.

Nakagawa Ichirō: A Uniquely Popular Trickster-Politician

Nakagawa Ichirō was born in 1925 in a bitterly cold, poverty-stricken, sparsely populated village in rural Hokkaidō, the northernmost island of Japan. With his mother in ill health and his father too austere to buy a magazine for his ten children, Nakagawa worked extraordinarily hard throughout his younger days to support the family. He was exceptionally good at the village school as well. He was the first person in his village to move on to secondary school. Vast areas of Hokkaidō had been and were in Nakagawa's younger days inhabited by poor immigrants from the mainland of Japan. Hokkaidō then was to a degree, Japan's counterpart to Siberia. After the central government became interested in developing Hokkaidō in the early Meiji, many of the immigrants were either criminals, failed lower-class samurai, or those desperate poor who saw no future on the mainland and took a bold chance. Nakagawa's family was among those poor immigrants who could afford neither rice nor electricity.

After graduating from Tokachi Agricultural School, he left Hok-kaidō for the mainland to enter the Junior Agricultural College in Utsunomiya, Gunma, a neighboring prefecture of Tokyo. As one of the top three students, he could move on to Kyūshū University. His persistent sympathy for peasants was such that he continued to choose agriculture as his major. Although he entered the bureaucracy upon graduation, he was not a career official nor did he have any intention of becoming a politician. It was only after he, as a low-rank-ing Hokkaidō Development Agency official, encountered the hope-less condition of rural peasants living in Hokkaidō and learned bitter lessons that a low-ranking official could do nothing to improve it that he began to consider becoming a politician. In his eyes, politicians were able to overpower the inflexible bureaucracy effectively. If he became a politician, he could bring to Hokkaidō a sufficiently large government subsidy for the fundamental improvement of agricul-ture, basically, a structural transformation into large-scale farming.

His first step toward the political world came with his appointment as private secretary to the director of the Hokkaidō Development Agency, Ōno Banboku, then a senior member of the ruling Liberal Democratic party. According to Nakagawa's own account, Ōno be-came interested in Nakagawa at Ōno's inaugural speech as the direc-tor of the agency. Nakagawa drew Ōno's attention because he was innocently sleeping in the front row while Ōno was speaking sol-emnly. After the inauguration party, Nakagawa was told to come to the new director's office. Contrary to his expectation, Ōno did not scold him for sleeping during his speech. Rather, Ōno, who had a magnanimous personality, became instantly fond of the unique mix-ture of innocence and boldness displayed by Nakagawa and asked him to become his secretary (Akasaka 1983, 302).

Ono became so fond of Nakagawa that he helped him successfully run for a Diet seat in 1963. Nakagawa was then thirty-eight years old, fairly young in the Japanese political tradition. Naturally, he joined Ōno's faction, but soon Ōno died. The faction split in two. Naka-gawa went along with Funada Naka, who parted company with Ōno's other lieutenant, Murakami Isamu. Funada's faction was the second smallest of the ten LDP factions of that day.[3]

The brief description of Nakagawa's career emphasizes that he re-ally had high potential to be an embodiment of liminal qualities. Hokkaidō where he was born and raised is, to begin with, a symbol-

[3] For biographical accounts on Nakagawa Ichirō, see Gendai Seiji Mondai Kenkyūkai (1979, 131–40); Watanabe (1974); Koike (1979); Nakagawa (1979); Koike and Group Q (1980); Naitō (1981); Nakano (1981); Shiibashi (1982); Akasaka (1983); and Tawara (1983).

ically, geographically, and culturally marginal land to the Japanese. The land historically was inhabited by criminals, dropouts, misfits, and the like. Its bitterly cold, rough climate and overwhelming wilderness had refused ordinary human beings—the persistent image of Hokkaidō. In addition to the marginality of his birthplace, his family's socioeconomic status was also marginal. They were poor immigrants from mainland Japan. They were continuously poor in the new wild frontier land. Not only the Nakagawas but also the entire village was poverty-stricken. Because of the severe cold of the long winter, Hokkaidō could not grow rice, the major staple food of the Japanese. Because the government had not been very enthusiastic about improving the situation in Hokkaidō, subsidies were always insufficient. Village houses were as meager as log huts without electricity.

Similarly, Nakagawa's academic background was in a marginal field. He never studied politics or law, which Japanese politicians usually choose. He studied agriculture throughout his school years. Even though he entered the bureaucracy, he had such a nonelite academic background and so little of an influential personal network that he started as a noncareer official of the Ministry of Agriculture, Forestry, and Fisheries. A young man like Nakagawa who was socially, economically, culturally, and educationally marginal could have had only the slenderest hope of becoming an influential political leader or even just a politician.

As mentioned, it was simply by luck that his and LDP senior politician Ōno Banboku's threads of fate crossed. Although he ultimately became a member of the ruling Liberal Democratic party thanks to Ōno's strong support, he originally had leaned towards the Japan Socialist party, especially its legendary leader Asanuma Inejirō, who was assassinated in October 1960. Nakagawa's favorite book throughout his life was *The Story of Poverty* written by the respected socialist, Kawakami Hajime (Gendai Seiji Mondai Kenkyūkai 1979, 133; Shiibashi 1982, 38). Even after he became an influential politician and an eminent presidential candidate of the LDP, Nakagawa showed his affinity with those marginally situated people who were poor, low in status, less educated, and so forth. Numerous episodes in Nakagawa's life in one way or another succinctly prove it.

These episodes also indicate that generally he was defiant of existing authority and free from established social and moral codes. In such stories, he appears as a figure who is unpredictable, extraordinarily energetic, one who challenges taboos, ridicules authorities, behaves rather vulgarly at times, and is quite emotional—becoming enraged like a steaming kettle, tenderly tearful, or laughing outright. Most of all, Nakagawa was the object of complex mixed feelings. He was adored and hated, yet exceptionally well tolerated by politicians of conservative and opposition parties alike, as well as the general public, reporters, bureaucrats, and even labor unionists and political critics. In other words, regardless of their socioeconomic status, or political ideology, people overwhelmingly had ambivalent feelings about him. All in all, he was a kind of person without whom people feel they have lost something substantial. A few episodes may help us picture what Nakagawa was really like.

Episodes in Nakagawa's Life as a Liminal Politician

EPISODE 1

When Nakagawa decided to run for the Diet seat he had nothing, that is, no money and no campaign headquarters but only Ōno's political endorsement. Nakagawa rented a room in a dairy farmer's house. Every morning he got up before six o'clock to clean his landlord's cow shed to pay his rent. One day he was late for a scheduled campaign speech in a tiny village because of heavy snow. When his truck was approaching the village, he jumped out of the truck to run, or more precisely, crawl toward the meeting hall. He looked like a snowman when he finally reached the door. Nakagawa, the Snowman, in his loudest voice apologized "S-O-O-O-RYY" to some ten people who had been waiting there. As soon as they saw Nakagawa and heard him thunderously apologize to them, they forgot their irritation. At one village hall, he made his campaign speech with his usual enthusiasm for over half an hour to an audience of one. This person became one of the most devoted Nakagawa supporters (Koike and Group Q 1980, 60).

After he won a remarkable victory at his first try—he gained the second largest number of votes despite being very young and new with no financial support or personal ties—a voluntary movement calling itself, "A Movement for Not Bothering Nakagawa Ichirō with Money Matters" was organized in Kushiro, a city of his constituency. The movement raised enough money to build a house for Nakagawa who could not afford to own his house then (Watanabe 1974, 93; Gendai Seiji Mondai Kenkyūkai 1979, 134–35).

EPISODE 2

Before he became a politician, Nakagawa, as a noncareer bureaucrat of the Hokkaidō Development Agency, had some bitter experiences with high-ranking officials in Tokyo. Frustrated with the impoverished living conditions of Hokkaidō peasants, Nakagawa, in meager

clothes and long rubber boots, went to Tokyo to ask for more adequate government subsidies. No relevant high-ranking official even
opened the door to him. Later, even after he became a minister, the
door of his office was always kept wide open (Gendai Seiji Mondai
Kenkyūkai 1979, 133–34). During my seven-month research period in
1983–1984 as an intern of another Diet member, I observed that
ninety-nine percent of the Diet members' office doors were kept
closed, if not locked. Nakagawa Ichirō had been unsurpassed in the
number of visitors he received per day among the Diet members. He
firmly kept to his philosophy that nobody was to be rejected. Nakagawa often jokingly said that the only kind of people whom he
would avoid were those who wanted to talk with a gun in their
hands. He went on to say that a sword or a club was all right because
he could escape by throwing his desk at the attacker (Koike and
Group Q 1980, 67).

On any given day, Nakagawa's office in the lower house building
had scarcely a moment without visitors. The hallway of the floor
where Nakagawa's office was located was popularly called "Nakagawa Ginza" (Ginza is Tokyo's busiest street). Sometimes he had
more than five hundred visitors a day in addition to his fellow Diet
members and their secretaries (of all parties), who constantly
stopped by his office just to say hello or to have a routine secretary-
to-secretary talk. Some of the visitors came from his constituency in
Hokkaidō and some were bureaucrats, whereas others were businessmen, newsmen, or people who just dropped in for a chat.
Many of them followed the Japanese custom and brought some gift,
often such famous local products as butter and cheese from Hokkaidō or oranges from the southern prefectures. All those gifts
were given to guards, cleaning women, operators, receptionists,
and drivers of the lower house and of his colleagues' offices (Koike
1979, 108). Nakagawa was extraordinarily popular among the various
service personnel. Yet, his unrivaled popularity did not simply rest
upon his gift giving; as veteran political journalist Koike pointed out
(Koike and Group Q 1980, 73), they, without calculation, just liked
him.

EPISODE 3

In his early days as a Diet member, Nakagawa was infamous for his
rough behavior. For example, while he was a member of the LDP's
Diet Policy Committee, he did not hesitate to show his impatience
with the oppositions' traditional Diet tactics of delaying a session by

all possible legal means, such as "cow-walking."[4] Nakagawa openly roared that he would no longer deal with the opposition and that he would rely on a snap vote. During the period following the late 1950's political turmoil that culminated in the U.S.-Japan Security Treaty Struggle in 1960, the Diet experienced the most violent, often physical, confrontations in postwar history. In Nakagawa's time, the Diet was still considerably prone to violence, if to a lesser degree.

During one such snap vote occasion, Nakagawa physically occupied the Well right below the lower house Speaker's podium, which overlooked the entire main hall, so that he could protect the Speaker from those opposition party members who might try to pull the Speaker down from his seat and thereby prevent the session from being held. Nakagawa was determined to remain there and during the struggles with the opposition members, he ripped a congresswoman's blouse (Gendai Seiji Mondai Kenkyūkai 1979, 136). Pushing, pulling, and elbowing were not, in those days, particularly outrageous in the Diet. Yet, those were the congressmen fighting with one another on the Diet floor. Congresswomen were, in Japanese culture, supposed to be kept outside the fight. Nakagawa's bold disregard of the cultural rule, therefore, was seen as outrageous and unforgivably rowdy even in the rough Diet period.

EPISODE 4

On the day in July 1976 when former prime minister Tanaka Kakuei was arrested in connection with the Lockheed scandal, Nakagawa was in his constituency in Hokkaidō, far away from Tokyo. That night, after he heard the news, he refused to sleep on his futon mattress, saying, "How can I sleep on a soft futon mattress when the person who once was our country's prime minister is kept in jail?" He slept directly on the hard wooden floor (Akasaka 1983, 303; Tawara 1983, 64–65). This most famous and most often cited story might not be precisely true, but it is important to recognize that regardless of its accuracy, people were ready to believe this kind of otherwise bizarre story as very Nakagawa-like. This attitude is especially significant because Nakagawa had been the loudest and most direct critic of Tanaka from the time Tanaka was at his peak.

EPISODE 5

While he was the director-general of the Science and Technology Agency in 1982, Nakagawa slipped out of the Diet session to go to

[4] See chap. 2 for a description of this tactic.

the backyard of the authoritative-looking Diet building, and there, in the open air, he urinated (Shiibashi 1982, 37). Unfortunately, a press photographer happened to capture the moment on film. The picture of him urinating circulated all over the country. The incident did not, however, lead to criticisms of him for amorality as a government minister or an influential member of the ruling party. His deed was popularly referred to for a while but not with feelings of serious disdain or anger. Instead, people giggled about it and called him "Oshikko daijin" (literally, minister pee-pee—the term, *oshikko* is very colloquial and is used only within an intimate group or among younger children). It seems more precise to say that the incident only helped him appear to be an unpredictable and lovable fellow among stark, somber, and pretentious politicians (Hosokawa 1982, 42; Shiibashi 1982, 37–38; "Girl Fridays" 1986).

In any case, it may be that dozens of his nicknames speak more eloquently than these episodes. No other politician was given as many nicknames as he. They included, "Devil's child" (Onikko), "Extreme right adventurist" (Uyoku bōkenshugisha), "Brown bear of the North Sea" (Hokkai no higuma), "Diet's rowdy kid" (Kokkai no abarenbō), "Hokkaidō potato" (Hokkaidōsan jagaimo), "Representative in a loincloth" (Fundoshi daigishi), "Rustic fellow representative" (Bankara daigishi), "Active hawk" (Kōdō takaha), and "Icchan" (an abridgment of his first name, Ichirō, like Bobby for Robert). Every name captures an essence of his nature. Together, they create a picture of a person who embodies all at the same time: a child (as opposed to an adult man), evil (as opposed to good), an untamed animal (as opposed to a human), ill-behaved (as opposed to disciplined), defiantly reckless (as opposed to reserved), and a poorly clothed barbarian (as opposed to a well-dressed civilized man).

Needless to say, the above terms in parentheses represent the characteristics that belong to nomos proper. These characteristics and values can secure their legitimacy and identity only by clearly defining and demarcating themselves from their complementary opposite, which, thus, are by necessity located at the margin of nomos. And Nakagawa, seen in the mirror of the Japanese people, embodies in full those qualities that are so unarguably a marginal being's. It is, therefore, not difficult to imagine that this trickster quality of Nakagawa is perceived as irresistible by a wide range of people in nomos.

Even such respected political critics as sharp-tongued Hosokawa Ryūgen and Fujiwara Hirotatsu could not help confessing that, despite all of Nakagawa's "notorious" deeds, they were charmed by him and highly valued his ability and potential. Hosokawa noted that even though Nakagawa looked like a blacksmith master with a brown bear–like rough, dark complexion, he attracted women as well as men and was highly valued among politicians (Hosokawa 1982, 142). Fujiwara gave his frank impression and evaluation of Nakagawa after he interviewed him. His comment is worth citing.

> (Nakagawa's) strong point derives from his stubborn and naive romanticism which appears very similar to that of Don Quixote among cunningly smart bureaucrat-turned politicians and shrewd strategist-politicians. . . .
>
> It was really refreshing to talk with him. He is definitely one kind of man whom I like. . . .
>
> I came to regard him as a sort of "Fool" (*Baka*) without whom no political drama can be played. . . .
>
> I think this role of "Fool" is invaluable to politics. . . .
>
> I am fairly convinced that the LDP-dominated political system in the eighties will be increasingly witnessing the phases in which "comedians" like Nakagawa play a crucial role in revitalizing it." (Fujiwara 1980, 134)

So far, we have laid out the argument that Nakagawa Ichirō had great potential to be a tricksterlike politician. And because of that inclination, he always caused this and that trouble in Japanese political life in a uniquely intriguing way. The troubles, which is a popular way to refer to the conditions brought about by the inherently deformative function of liminal qualities embodied in Nakagawa, allowed for the possibility of a broad, fundamental change. Even if such a change did not occur, the trickster quality of Nakagawa at least provided ordinary people with opportunities to reexamine their whole worlds, including their analyses of themselves, their relationships with others, and existing arrangements. That examination, in turn, helped people keep themselves from complete reification.

The Seirankai

The first big trouble caused by Nakagawa was in July 1973, when he, with thirty younger LDPs, formed a transfactional group, the Seirankai, Young Storm Society. *Seiran* refers to an early summer storm that stirs young green leaves and sweeps away all the dirt of this world. With this name, the group hoped to cause a refreshing stir in what many critics considered to be a stagnated ruling LDP (Akiyama 1973, 10; "Seirankai" 1974, 44).

These thirty-one members had one peculiarly noticeable characteristic in common—marginality in every respect. First, they were young in terms of political age (number of times elected) as well as biological age. None had been elected more than four times, and their average age was 47.5 years. It is a tacit rule in the LDP that any member can climb a ladder that leads to a post of minister, in principle, as he or she adds political age. With an electoral survival of two or three terms, an LDP member would be appointed political vice-minister. When a member's political age reaches five or six times, he or she is considered ready for a ministerial post. Almost all members of adequate political age could and should experience a ministerial or vice-ministerial post at least once. Because in Japan's political system the cabinet is usually reshuffled several times under one prime minister, new positions are available constantly.

This practice works so naturally and is so much taken for granted that if a member has not experienced ministership after the political age of eight, for example, the case becomes news to the major newspapers. Indeed one unfortunate person added a tenth political term after the June 1980 election with no ministership, largely owing to a series of bad luck—wrong time, wrong faction, wrong kind of ties, and so forth. Besides being often referred to in informal Nagatachō conversations, a major newspaper featured him in an article that carried a large (2.4" × 3.5") portrait.[5]

As for biological age, which is far less important than the number of times elected, the Seirankai members' average age of 47.5 years was fairly young in the Japanese political context. A political career in Japan is quite often one's second pursuit. That is, the ordinary course for a politician in Japan is first to become either a career bureaucrat at a major ministry, a successful businessman, a local politician, or some influential politician's secretary. Only after having gathered sufficient financial power, personal ties, and political endorsement while working for years as a bureaucrat, businessman, political secretary, local politician, and the like, could one be ready to run for the Diet—as soon as one gets a constituency either by taking over from a retiring or dead politician or forcefully squeezing oneself into it.

There are those who may choose a political career as their first and often lifelong vocation. They are the second-generation politicians, who include not only sons and daughters of a politician parent but also sons-in-law, brothers and sisters, and other relatives. They can afford to run for Diet seats at a relatively younger age because they *inherit* everything intact from the first-generation politicians, for example, well-established names, personal networks, financial power, and the constituencies.[6] In any case, with the Japanese retirement

---

[5] *Mainichi Shimbun*, Dec. 1, 1983.

[6] It is important to note here that so far we have been talking about Liberal Democratic party politicians. The rules and practices described can by no means be applied to the opposition parties. Diet members from the Japan Socialist party, for example,

age around fifty-five or sixty, freshman politicians in their fifties are not unusual. In this light, the Seirankai members' average age was quite notable, especially when we discover that only three second-generation politicians were among them.

Second, none belonged to the then mainstream factions: the Tanaka Kakuei and Ōhira Masayoshi.[7] When Seirankai were formed in 1973, there were five major and four minor factions and eleven independents (see table 4.1). Under Tanaka's premiership, the Tanaka and Ōhira factions formed the mainstream coalition with their combined numerical superiority. The Seirankai consisted of three almost even-sized groupings. Twelve members belonged to the faction of Fukuda Takeo, chief adversary of Tanaka; nine derived from the faction of Nakasone Yasuhiro (who had acquired the unpleasant nickname of "weathervane" because of his *amoral*, distrustful political behavior); the remaining ten belonged either to minor factions or to none.

To belong to no faction or to minor or nonmainstream factions means that chances to climb up the ladder smoothly are low. That is, even though everyone, regardless of his or her faction, could occupy a ministerial post at least once, often the ministerial post is not as prestigious as Finance, Foreign Affairs, or International Trade and Industry. It is least likely for minor faction members or independents to become a prime minister. In other words, these Seirankai members were situated farthest from the power center and, thus, had the least to hope for.

This characteristic will be further articulated when Seirankai academic backgrounds and previous professional careers are studied. To become a career bureaucrat who could later move into the political world smoothly, it was almost a prerequisite to have graduated from Japan's unrivaled and prestigious University of Tokyo. Naturally, the

may start their careers as unionists of the General Council of Japan Labor Unions. Or, in the middle-of-the-road party, Kōmeitō, Diet members are heavily drawn from its backbone, the neo-Buddhist sect, Sōka Gakkai.

[7] Mainstream factions refer to the ones by which the post of prime minister/party president and key Cabinet and/or party positions are held. Because the Liberal Democratic party has been enjoying the majority from its formation in 1955, the LDP president automatically becomes prime minister as well. In its early days, factions in the LDP were in much more conflictual relationships, so antimainstream factions were completely excluded from both cabinet and party executive posts. From the sixties, after the unprecedented political turmoil caused by the U.S.–Japanese Security Treaty under the Kishi Nobusuke government, an accommodationist trend has prevailed so posts are allocated according to the numerical size of each faction. It is, therefore, more appropriate to call those factions that do not constitute the core of the government nonmainstream instead of antimainstream.

TABLE 4.1
Factions in the LDP in 1973

Faction	Members
Fukuda Takeo	56
Tanaka Kakuei	48
Ōhira Masayoshi	45
Miki Takeo	37
Nakasone Yasuhiro	36
Shiina Etsusaburō	18
Mizuta Mikio	13
Funada Naka	12
Ishii Mitsujirō	10
Independents	13

Source: Nihon Seikei Shimbunsha (Feb. 1973, 46: 341–43).

proportion of the Tokyo University graduates in the LDP (as well as in some other opposition parties, notably, the Japan Communist party) is extremely high. In 1973, 86 of the total of 274 LDP representatives had graduated from the University of Tokyo. Among twenty-six Representatives of the Seirankai, only two were Tokyo University graduates; the remaining five Seirankai members were Councilors, none of whom had graduated from Tokyo University either. That is, we see a stark difference in the academic backgrounds of the two groups: 31.4 percent of the LDP representatives were Tokyo University graduates, whereas as few as 7.7 percent of the Seirankai representatives had graduated from that university.

One significant but quite natural consequence is that no top bureaucrats-turned-politicians were in the Seirankai. To be sure, former bureaucrats did join the Seirankai; there were, as a matter of fact, six of them. However, they belonged to local agencies or, in the major central ministries, they were on sidetracks that would not lead to the upper echelons of the bureaucracy. Two former career bureaucrats of the Finance Ministry had resigned at the lower level of a bureaucratic ladder long before entering politics as influential politicians' private secretaries.

As neither second-generation nor Tokyo University graduate-elite bureaucrats nor successful businessmen, the Seirankai members were very much like self-help frontiersmen. Fourteen of them managed to work closely with Diet members as secretaries, using that career as an effective springboard toward the political world. Not only did it provide a valuable learning opportunity but also a crucial chance to take over the constituency. Even if such a golden chance did not come, a Diet member's secretary in Japanese politics is much more like a lieutenant to the politician, or even sometimes an acting Diet member, so that each could develop personal and financial networks among politicians, bureaucrats, and businessmen for future use.

Another former major career held by as many as eight Seirankai members was that of local politician. They moved on from a tiny constituency, such as a village, to town, to city, to prefecture, and eventually reached national level. As either Diet members' secretaries or local politicians, their roads toward the Diet seats were never as smooth as those of the elite bureaucrats, second-generation politicians, or business elite. Twenty-two of the thirty-one Seirankai members, 71 percent, had traveled rocky roads. To survive, they commonly had to be independent and shrewd and had to challenge existing authorities.

As exemplified in a leader of the group, Nakagawa Ichirō, some of the Seirankai members had already drawn the attention of their Diet colleagues as well as the media and political critics because of their, in one way or another, extraordinary behavior and activities on and off the Diet floor. For example, during the Diet debate, one member not only raised his voice to the level of a thunder drum but also abusively disclosed an opposition member's private scandal, including both false and true allegations. Another member appeared on a television program, spoke at a convention, and wrote an article urging the nation to abandon the peace clause of the constitution. In the context of an overwhelmingly pacifist postwar Japanese culture, it was almost taboo to urge military buildup and to advocate abandoning the no-war clause of the constitution. Some members' overt, eccentric, and extraordinary behavior, combined with their general association with hawkish Fukuda and Nakasone factions, contributed to the establishment of their notorious reputation as vulgar marginals. As such, to ordinary LDP members, they did not deserve serious attention although the group sometimes caused them eyebrow-knitting embarrassment.

In this section, we will take a close look at a dramatic political rite of passage that helped make the young, vulgar marginals appear to be dedicated and pure-spirited leaders of the new generation. The rites of passage took place on the hot and humid night of July 10, 1973, in a prestigious Tokyo hotel room. Men in formal dark suits gathered around the table. On it were the traditional Japanese *suzuribako* (a decorated box for a brush writing kit containing a *sumi* ink slab, ink stone, and a couple of brushes) and the pure white Japanese paper that is used on special occasions. The six-article "Blood Oath" was written in traditional sumi ink with brush. It reads:

> The Liberal Democratic party has achieved remarkable prosperity from the ashes of the war defeat. Nonetheless, we are witnessing various problems, such as extraordinary inflation and pollution, which the high economic growth policy has inevitably generated. We will make every effort to improve the situation. At the same time we are firmly determined to accomplish a fundamental reform of the party and politics in general by reviving the party's original founding spirit while striking a warning drum loudly at high pitch to make other LDP members realize the urgent crisis. No external pressure will crush our determination. Our strong comradeship transcends factional division so that our actions can incorporate a broad range of points of view of the Japanese nation-state and Japanese race.
>
> We are firmly convinced that is the historical mission we are given.

THE BLOOD OATH

> 1. We support a free society. Our foreign policy principle is to solidify and maintain close linkage with free nations.
>
> 2. To exalt Japanese traditional morals, we will correct the current social trend of materialism and normalize the educational system as well.
>
> 3. We respect labor. We have sympathy for poor and unfortunate people. To establish new social justice, we will correct the present unfair distribution of wealth and eliminate unlabored income.
>
> 4. We will urge the nation toward the necessity of national defense and security to construct a peace state. We will keep ourselves very active on this issue.
>
> 5. We will create Japan's own independent Constitution in order to achieve genuine freedom, security, and prosperity for the Japanese race in the new era.
>
> 6. With respect to the management of the Liberal Democratic Party, we will destroy such evil old customs and practices as easy, unprincipled compromises, bureaucratism, and opportunism.

FINAL WORDS

> The members of the Seirankai swear with blood to accomplish all of the above. Every Seirankai member dedicates his own life to take action toward that objective rather than engage in endless, unconstructive arguments while remaining inactive. (Minato and the Seirankai 1974, 190–91)

On the table waited also a brand-new razor. That the ritual of blood oath was to take place had been strictly secret. Only the twenty-four participants were supposed to know about it. The air in the room had come to be so tense that the very simple deed of cutting one's little finger (some tried to cut a thumb) could not be done smoothly. One by one, passing one razor, they eventually managed to generate a drop of pure red blood to stamp below their names on the paper.[8]

On July 17, 1973, by which time, the number of the members had increased to thirty-one, a leader, Nakagawa Ichirō read aloud the "Blood Oath" to the crowded press conference called to announce formally the Seirankai formation. The foreign press[9] as well as a large corps of domestic news media were drawn to the press conference. A blood oath, like *seppuku*—to kill oneself by cutting one's abdomen with a sword—is Japan's traditional ritual to show participants' purity, sincerity, and unshakable loyalty to what was decided. It binds all participants with unbreakable, sacred bonds, so that no one would withdraw from or betray the union made. The blood oath was not rare in the Middle Ages among commoners, peasants as well as samurai, on such occasions as launching a rebellion.[10] In modern Japanese society, the blood oath is an almost forgotten tradition, however. Only in the underground world of gangs is that tradition said to be still surviving.

The immediate reaction of the media, political critics, and politicians was a mixture of fear, contempt, sarcasm, and annoyance. They were afraid because they thought the loud-voiced, extremist rebels would pull the country toward the familiar road to fascism. They were contemptuous because they interpreted the Seirankai members as little more than aggressive, vulgar young turks. They were sarcastic because they considered the blood oath ritual not only anachronistic but also superficial nonsense because they used a razor blade instead of the traditional Japanese sword.[11]

Much criticism, many raised eyebrows, and ridicule followed the Seirankai formation, and increased as the blood oath takers showed on various political issues that they were really serious about what they swore with blood. It is very important to notice that, along with the negative reactions, the Seirankai attracted a wide range of enthusiastic supporters, secret admirers, and sympathizers. *Asahi Shimbun* editorial staff writer Tominomori Eiji noted that he heard one young

[8] The description of the ritual night is based on Tawara's (1978b) account.

[9] See *Newsweek*, "The Razor-Blade Oath," July 30, 1973, p. 37.

[10] One variation of blood oath taking was a ritual of sacred water drinking before the Shintoist god(s), and its significant meaning and function was exactly the same as that of the blood oath. For examples of such symbolic, solidifying rituals on the eve of a rebellion in the Middle Ages in Japan, see Wakamori (1944); Watanabe S. (1945); Hayashiya (1951); Aida (1962:920–25, 2:565–68); and Yokoi (1975).

[11] For criticisms of the Seirankai's blood oath ritual, radical philosophy, and policy principles, see Ishikawa (1973); comments by University of Tokyo emeritus professor Horigome Yōzō and critic-editor Yamamoto Natsuhiko on the Seirankai in *Asahi Shimbun*, July 19, 1973, p. 22; "Rankiryū" (1974); and Watanabe T. (1974).

Diet member reflectively say, "I felt for the first time in my life I have become a politician when I participated in the Seirankai-sponsored meeting." The young Diet member had been critical of part of the Seirankai's political philosophy and deeds; however, serious discussions at the Seirankai meeting could not help but impress him deeply. He felt fresh political vitality grasp his heart (Tominomori 1974, 242–43).

I was told a similarly reminiscent story by one Diet member's official secretary with whom I had been working for seven months at the Diet office between 1983 and 1984. This secretary was about thirty when the Seirankai was formed. He was just an ordinary Diet member's secretary—gentle, talkative, and always well groomed. He said that despite their frequent excesses in deeds and words, he was gradually attracted by the Seirankai. When the Seirankai held its first "People's Grand Oratory Convention" in January 1974 at Nippon Budōkan (a gigantic hall for traditional Japanese martial arts matches), he was among the enthusiastic twenty-six thousand participants, the largest in Nippon Budōkan's history—no other political group had ever drawn that many participants before. At the convention, he was overwhelmed with a feeling of exaltation. He truly believed that he could do something noble for the country, for the higher human cause (LDP Diet member Watanuki Tamisuke's official secretary Iwanade Yoshitaka).

At that convention, the Seirankai approved a declaration stating that if Prime Minister Tanaka did not correct his policy to assure less fortunate people fair treatment, the Seirankai would demand Tanaka's resignation and devote their lives to achieve that end ("Jimin AA-ken" 1974). In this period, few politicians dared criticize Prime Minister Tanaka so directly, explicitly, and openly. The public still liked the rare commoner-premier who graduated from neither university nor high school.[12] Furthermore, to most LDP members, juniors and seniors alike, to appear an outright opponent of Tanaka was, at the least, disadvantageous in terms of financial support, political endorsement, and post allocation. Thus, although many politicians did not completely agree with Tanaka's policies, they generally remained only private critics. In those circumstances, Nakagawa Ichirō, leading the Seirankai, was almost the sole critic with such directness of the powerful, often called "one man" or "computer-run bulldozer" premier (Naitō 1981, 244).

[12] For Tanaka Kakuei's upbringing and political career, see the following section on Tanaka; also for an interesting comparison of careers of commoner-premier Tanaka and his chief rival and elite bureaucrat-turned-premier Fukuda Takeo, see Calder (1982).

Attack on the powerful aside, the Seirankai's active, taboo-breaking way of handling various political issues attracted constant attention. For example, the LDP's annual convention in mid-January 1974 was startled by a Seirankai member who brought a microphone into the convention hall to disrupt the speakers with loud heckling. A freshman LDP who attended the convention complained later that the blaring heckling wiped out speeches and its rough language truly frightened the faint-hearted (Yamashita 1974, 131). Participants at the same party convention were shocked again by another Seirankai member when he made an unexpected speech, radical in tone, that called on the party to return to its founding spirit, that is, to replace the U.S.–imposed constitution with Japan's own. The speech shook the entire convention because the LDP, since the period under premier Ikeda Hayato in 1960, had stopped advocating constitutional revision officially; instead, the party had been putting major emphasis on higher economic growth. In other words, economic policy had been given top priority since 1960. Accordingly, the annual LDP conventions had not particularly referred to that clause of the party platform for more than a decade.

Two Seirankai-caused incidents totally altered an otherwise very peaceful, smooth, orderly ceremony. In fact, despite the LDP rule stipulating that the annual convention is the highest institution for party decision making,[13] it is by no means more than a festive, ceremonial occasion. It is popularly and quite adequately called a "shan shan" convention. "Shan shan" is the sound of a special, auspicious way of clapping hands together when something is agreed upon and all are happy about it. From my experience at the January 1984 LDP annual convention, I can easily imagine how truly startled attendants of the 1974 convention were by such totally unexpected and disruptive incidents. The 1984 convention was, like most of its predecessors, a mixture of a very merry festive, ceremonial mood with an air of solemn, formal ritual. Proceedings were quite orderly throughout, and ended with a thunderous chorus of "Jimintō *Banzai! Banzai! Banzai!*" by all participants with their hands both raised high during each of the three shouts. At the 1974 convention, the Seirankai brought chaos into the order and forcefully reminded all participants of the originally intended function of the annual party convention, and thereby revealed to them an empty formality, or limitation, in established convention procedure.

As exemplified in this case, the Seirankai members in various issues brought destructive elements into the taken-for-granted wisdom

---

[13] Liberal Democratic Party Rule, chap. 3, ART. 29 (Jiyū Minshutō 1983, 10).

and practice of political life. In so doing, they upset those who in one way or another constituted an existing moral order and authority. Naturally, the Seirankai invited considerable, emotionally charged criticism. As a matter of fact, almost all books and articles that deal with the Seirankai's unpredictable, taboo-breaking behavior and activities contain unusually emotional and lopsided attacks on the Seirankai by critics, journalists, and both the conservative and opposition party members.[14]

Still, the peculiarly appealing power of the Seirankai could not help but attract not only people generally, as shown in its twenty-six thousand-participant "People's Grand Oratory Convention" but also those LDP seniors and executives, including most conspicuously, the prime minister himself. Within five months from its formation in July 1973, the Seirankai had two meetings with Tanaka. The first meeting was as early as July 26 and lasted more than 1.5 hours so that the Speaker of the upper house, whose appointment with the premier was scheduled to follow, had to be kept in a waiting room. Twenty Seirankai members led by Nakagawa had a frank discussion about their basic beliefs, ideals, and policies with the prime minister whom they had been openly attacking. Tanaka, interestingly enough, not only agreed to meet them face-to-face but also rather enjoyed it. After the meeting, Tanaka told reporters, "Their passion derives from purest patriotism. They are studying a broad range of issues quite well." He also sympathized with the Seirankai with such compassionate comment that he was convinced that young members' direct and open criticisms of party policies and management had contributed to the improvement of the LDP throughout its history. He said that he himself was once one of those young turks.[15]

In the second meeting, the Seirankai made a direct policy request to Prime Minister Tanaka. The Seirankai urged strongly that the government give utmost priority to the inflation policy for the next year, 1974. Prime minister Tanaka who was then well known for not acknowledging inflation acceleration, at least partly, by his policy of "Restructuring the Japanese Archipelago," was provoked, and the two sides engaged in heated debate. Or, more adequately put, as Seirankai member Watanabe Michio later described it, the Seirankai's outright challenge to the premier's basic policy drew both sides into heated *kenka* arguments (Utsumi et al. 1973, 23).

Kenka, Watanabe's term, has a very amicable and informal conno-

---

[14] See, for example, "Jimintō tandoku de" (1973); "Fuan to shōryo" (1974); Hosojima (1974); Iwami (1974); "Rankiryū" (1974); "Tokyo-hatsu Peking-bin" (1974); Watanabe T. (1974); and "Yasukuni Jinja" (1974).

[15] *Ashai Shimbun*, July 27, 1973, p. 2.

tation that refers generally to in-family fights between sisters and/or brothers, and between friends, or children; in other words, kenka is fought by those who are in a very close relationship and know that the quarrel will soon be over without damage to their relationship. It must be noticed here that the Seirankai, whose members had been insignificant, negligible marginals before its formation with the blood oath, was now in a position to make direct policy recommendations in addition to having rather intimate face-to-face meetings with the prime minister. This exceptional tolerance by an authority seems to be exactly the same kind that a king used to show to his court jester, one of the various trickster figures. Like a court jester, the Seirankai members were in no legitimate position within the institutional arrangements of nomos that would allow them to request the prime minister to listen to their criticisms in an exclusive exchange. In other words, their direct access to the core of authority was through the interstices of nomos.

Another intriguing fact is that the Seirankai, a group of formerly heterogeneous marginals, constantly sent several of its members to important party and cabinet posts rapidly, not just one at a time. In November 1973, only four months after the group's formation, Tanaka appointed five Seirankai members as political vice-ministers: Nakagawa Ichirō (four-termer), Watanabe Michio (four-termer), Morishita Motoharu (three-termer), Utsumi Hideo (three-termer), and Kusunoki Masatoshi (two-term councilor). All five were in major ministries, such as Finance, International Trade and Industry, and Construction. As Satō and Matsuzaki (1986, 39) in their meticulous study point out, it was usual to appoint two- to four-termers as vice-ministers and, therefore, the political age of these five Seirankai members was considered to be just right, not unusual. Still, the appointments could not help but draw attention from the media and the general public as well as other LDP members.[16] One-fourth of the total of twenty vice-minister posts went to the Seirankai at one time. In the next cabinet reshuffle under Tanaka Kakuei in November 1974, another five Seirankai members were appointed as political vice-ministers: Yamazaki Heihachirō, Etō Takami, Kokuba Kōshō, Nakayama Masaaki, and Nakamura Kōkai, all two-termers.

The people's perception of and attitudes toward the Seirankai were, surely, hatred, contempt, embarrassment, anger, and the like. Yet, the truth about attitudes toward the Seirankai as revealed by various media interviews with other opposition as well as conservative party members, bureaucrats, political critics, journalists, business-

---

[16] See, for example, Utsumi et al. (1973).

men, and labor unionists is that virtually everyone liked them or found the Seirankai members, especially Nakagawa Ichirō, irresistible. One who was peculiarly attracted by the Seirankai and Nakagawa was Fujiwara Hirotatsu, a respected university professor turned political critic.[17] Matsuzaki Yoshinobu, managing director of the Japan Federation of Employers' Association, noted:

> Unlike most of the politicians, the Seirankai members are not afraid of provoking the mass media, which is powerful enough to be called popularly the fourth branch of the government. They are really interesting fellows. I hope they will continue this way even when they get older, without becoming like the present leadership. (Inose, Sano, and Yamane 1978, 136)

Kōno Yōhei, who in 1976 left the LDP with five others to form their own New Liberal Club, and whose political philosophy was popularly known to be diametrically opposed to that of Nakagawa and the Seirankai, said of Nakagawa:

> He understands warm human emotion extremely sensitively. He is peerless in charming people. I am sure that he will be one of the most prominent leaders of the Liberal Democratic party. (Nakagawa Ichirō 1979, 100)

The Socialist mayor of Obihiro, Hokkaidō, Yoshimura Hiroshi, reflected:

> He is, almost by nature, able to build an intimate relationship with people. Since he is always so earnest, nobody can resist. He has something irresistible in him. (Koike and Group Q 1980, 59)

And Miyashita Sōhei, an elite bureaucrat at the Finance Ministry, now an LDP politician, stated:

> "Icchan" tends to act out of intuition (*chokkan*) rather than calculation (*keisan*). Generally, bureaucrats are quite skillful, with huge volumes of statistics and logic, in refuting congressmen's requests to increase the budget to this or that particular project. But, bureaucrats of the Finance Ministry almost unconditionally accept Nakagawa's requests. "Icchan" is a man of sincerity and affection whose popularity in the Finance Ministry is absolutely unrivaled (Koike and Group Q 1980, 59–60)

Tomizuka Mitsuo, secretary-general of the General Council of Japan Labor Unions, said:

> If we made him angry, Nakagawa would be unmanageable. But when we sincerely and frankly talk with him, we can reach a deep, mutual understanding regardless of the ideological differences. He makes numerous

---

[17] See Fujiwara (1980, 134) for his comment on Nakagawa.

friends with those in the opposition camp through such a sincere and frank attitude. (Naitō 1981, 254)

Two prominent journalists expressed their frank amazement at finding an unusually favorable evaluation of and feeling towards Nakagawa and the Seirankai among members of the opposition parties as well as the LDP:

Curiously, Nakagawa is valued rather highly among the LDPs. His unique mixture of emotional, sincere, and magnanimous characteristics is quite precious and hard to find nowadays.[18]

I was surprised when I found a quite high evaluation of the Seirankai during my research of and interviews with LDP members. Moreover, such high evaluation is not limited to the LDP but extends to the opposition parties.[19]

Moreover, the Seirankai members have been outstandingly successful when running for election. In other words, they are very popular in their constituencies. For instance, Nakagawa Ichirō gained an unrivaled number of votes in every election except his first try, as mentioned. Even an ever-controversial member, such as Hamada Kōichi, former member of a real gang, has been unarguably strong in elections.[20]

Discussion

Individually insignificant, marginal politicians gathered together and took a secret blood oath ritual. In the postritual period, these individuals, formerly with negligible hope, intruded onto the center stage through interstices of the structures. It is conspicuous that few of those who are either critical of, or sympathetic with, the Seirankai seem to be aware of the fact that they themselves may have changed their perception of, and attitude towards, these young men after the blood oath ritual. They also seem to be unaware that the Seirankai members have acquired a new identity by undergoing that ritual. That the process of a ritual alters a subject's identity and others' attitude toward the subject is a well-established academic premise in

---

[18] Iwami Takao (1977, 137) the political section staff writer of the *Mainichi Shimbun*.

[19] See the comments of the noted free-lancer, Tawara Sōichirō (1978a, 198).

[20] He won eight elections: town level twice, prefectural level twice, and national level four times. He lost only once at the national level at the age of thirty-two when he attempted to leap from town to national level. It was from the outset regarded as too adventurous. For a detailed description of Hamada's election style, see Shiota and Magami (1980, especially, 126–44).

symbolic anthropology. As Leach (1967) points out, symbolic behavior *does* something as well as *says* something, although the latter function is more popularly acknowledged. Blood letting, tear shedding, tooth extracting, hair-removing, circumcising, and the like are public symbolism whose source derives from a collective cultural rule, not private psychology.

Through these forms of ritual symbolism, an individual undergoes ritual cleansing, that is, the subject is separated from former profane qualities and made to transfer to another state of being (Leach 1967). Most significantly, the change is accepted as the nature of things; hence the resulting situation has an absolute legitimacy because it derives from cosmos. Legitimacy that is built within the domain of nomos, in contrast, is considered to be on fragile ground. Any one cosmos can offer multiple interpretations and points of view for people's lives in nomos, whereas only another cosmos (rather than nomos) can challenge the existing cosmos.[21] In other words, more than one legitimacy in nomos is possible within the scope of one cosmos. Consequently, it can be logically argued that a nomos-based legitimacy is not only ubiquitous but also replaceable with another relatively easily.

In contrast, changes resulting from a transitional ritual process, which as Terrence Turner (1977) analyzes, essentially involves cosmos as well as nomos dimensions, appear natural to people because they accompany a new cosmos-oriented organizational principle of elements of nomos. The difference between nomos-based and cosmos-oriented changes may be pictured when we think, for example, of the tremendous difficulty involved in enforcing Christian-oriented, Western-valued marriage law on an Islamic society. Imposing a new law is an activity in nomos. Especially in this case, the Christian-oriented marriage law has little to do with the Islamic people's cosmos. What about the fact that a wedding ritual, not a marriage law, can do much to create a full-fledged member of the society in an hour or so? In a wedding ritual, a female subject transforms from an immature girl into an adult woman after undergoing the liminal phase. There, elements that accompanied her old girlhood merge with another set of elements attached to an adult woman/wife to produce her unique new identity, which simultaneously involves changes in others' attitude towards, and perception of, her.

The same transformation, it can be assumed, took place during the Seirankai's blood oath ritual. On the one hand, we see those men

---

[21] On this point, see Kuhn (1970); Itō (1974, 39); Ueno (1977, 117); also Popper (1959, 1970) and Brown (1979).

who were marginal in educational background, socioeconomic status, and both political and biological age. On the other hand, we have pure-spirited young patriots, *Yūkoku no shishi* as they have frequently been referred to after the ritual. *"Yūkoku no shishi"* literally means pure-spirited samurai who devote themselves to the country, and the term usually referred to those younger, lower-class local samurai who contributed enormously to the history of the catastrophic last days of the Edo period that gave birth to the new Meiji era. Youth, political inexperience, status-marginality, and defiance of the existing order now are interpreted as purity, unselfishness, and freedom from the present ill-functioning system and its holders' influence.

Before the blood oath ritual, the relationship between the men of the Seirankai and the LDP executives, for instance, may be described as one between vulgar misfits and well-restrained power holders. This relationship was changed, however. At the perceptual level, vulgar misfits turned into courageous challengers to the stagnated old establishment, motivated by their pure-spirited patriotism. Together with the media, people began calling them "Yūkoku no shishi." To call them by a different name is no insignificant matter. What they are called reflects how people interpret and perceive them and their deeds. Banging a fist on the desk, for instance, had been interpreted previously as the ruffian deed of a lowly politician, yet the same action could be seen now as an expression of patriotic zeal.[22]

Calling them "Yūkoku no shishi"—an instant reminder of the great Meiji revolutionaries in the great national crisis—was inevitably accompanied by another significant change in people's view in the Japanese collective cultural rule. It indicates that they unconsciously acknowledged that some evil existed in the system and that the present authority was not only ill-equipped but also deserved criticism of its fundamental principle and course. In a word, superior justice is always on the side of the "Yūkoku no shishi" in national crises in the Japanese cultural context. The members became attached to this new identity that was radically different from the old one they had shaken off through the ritual. These men of liminal qualities with new identities as pure-spirited patriots forcefully brought in inconsistencies. At the time when the country's priority was economic, material prosperity, the Seirankai's blood oath ritual counterposed another set of

---

[22] In this connection, see Fernandez's (1972, 1977) argument that "metaphoric assertions men make about themselves or about others influence their behavior" (Fernandez 1972, 42).

values and principles that was based on spiritualism and Japan's indigenous egalitarianism.

As a consequence, existing institutional arrangements, moral and value standards, classifications of matters, things and people appeared ambiguous or lost exclusive legitimacy. The Seirankai lacked concrete and coherent policies. It was their abstract spiritualism that drew people from such an extremely broad range of categories. This indicates that, thanks to inconsistencies brought in by the Seirankai and the consequent deformation of existing institutional arrangements, people had an opportunity to reexamine their states of being and to distance themselves from their previously undoubted commitments. That is, people's reflexivity became activated.

Our theoretical point of view suggests that one's intention and/or intended outcome as well as one's position in the social structure (in the Marxist sense) may not necessarily be relevant when we consider power as something that involves change in all cosmos, nomos, and chaos. Moreover, we are made to recognize that one's possessions, such as high socioeconomic status, white skin, better educational background, and so forth, would not by themselves make one superior in bringing about the possibilities of genuine change. From our standpoint, one who has a socioeconomically and culturally marginal status, is less educated, and has those attributes that are generally regarded in modern times as disadvantageous (such as darker skin and non-European languages) could be seen to be superior in this potential to white-skinned, European-tongued elites. It can be argued, in line with Shils (1975), that the elite who are situated in the socio-cultural-economic-political center are too committed themselves to the existing central value system to realize a huge range of symbols. In other words, they can see only a very limited range of symbols.

In contrast, those marginals whose commitment to the existing central value–symbol system is rather loose can see destructive, substantially revolutionary—that is, absolutely incompatible with the existing system—symbols. Regardless of their intention, they cannot help but ceaselessly shake the existing value system by counterposing fundamentally irreconcilable elements. Once a given symbol system occupies the center, it has no choice but to start to concentrate its efforts on defending itself against incompatible, challenging symbol systems lurking in a marginal sphere. It is unlikely, in other words, given a very limited scope of available (so perceived) symbols, that the center can recreate and regenerate itself by picking up a certain substantially destructive as well as incompatible symbol system. Hence, the most likely course would be the one in which the initiative of change is in the hands of the bearers of the marginal symbol systems.

In any event, power—defined as having a potential that allows for the condition in which genuine three-dimensional change is possible—lies most likely with liminal qualities. In addition, power has very little to do with the initiator's intention or intended outcome. A symbol's inevitable nature of ambiguity must invite an unpredictable and mutually unrelated chain of occurrences. A sole key to the concept of power, in our view, concerns an ability to deform and relativize any taken-for-granted worldview. And this is what we have seen in the experiences of a trickster-like politician, Nakagawa Ichirō, and his fellow Seirankai members.

Tanaka Kakuei and Nakasone Yasuhiro: Deformers at the Center

Embodiment of liminal qualities can be found even at the core of the structures. What V. Turner ([1969] 1977:128) wrote two decades ago still has validity. He argued: "Communitas breaks in through the interstices of structure, in liminality: at the edge of structure, in marginality; and from beneath structure in inferiority." That is, major holders of nomos institutions are by no means immune to the deformative quality of liminality. They, too, experience moments of becoming marginal beings or entering liminal states. They are not exceptions; they have a chance to embody liminal qualities under certain temporal and spatial conditions.

These liminal experiences that all people share regardless of their roles and statuses in nomos are not always compatible with what the Weberian might think of charisma. As discussed in the introductory chapter, charisma's *transformative* quality contrasts with the *deformative* quality of liminality. Charisma possesses and originates its own consistent worldview. With this original worldview, charisma arouses and leads ordinary people. In a word, charisma imposes a particular alternative worldview from outside upon the context in order to transform it.

Liminal qualities that can break in anywhere to be embodied by any kind of people and matter, including those situated at the center of the institutional structures, deform context from within. Marginal beings and liminal states inherently lack a consistent worldview because of their inevitable dualism. They, by nature, cannot originate or impose any systematic, internally consistent worldview. Liminality refuses any coherent, accomplished worldview. Liminality, in short, is accompanied by unconditional deformation.

It then may be argued that besides the Weberian notion of transformative change brought about from the outside by charisma, there could be another kind. That is, those who bear the center of nomos and ordinary people equally experience moments of liminal states and embody liminal qualities under certain conditions. All that would contribute to the deformation of the context from within. In other words, owing to the deformative function of indiscriminately embodied and ubiquitously experienced liminality, even the center of nomos institutions may well have a potential for self-destruction/ regeneration. In the following section, two of Japan's most outstanding and most controversial political leaders—former prime ministers Tanaka Kakuei and Nakasone Yasuhiro—will be observed to embody liminal qualities.

Tanaka Kakuei

Tanaka Kakuei, who became prime minister in July 1972 at the age of fifty-four was the fifth youngest premier in Diet history since the Meiji Restoration in 1867 (Jyōhō Kenkyūsho 1983, 29). His entire career can be seen as a defiance of and challenge to the established order. He came from a poor family in a rural region of the snowy northeast prefecture, Niigata, and graduated neither from high school nor university. It was, rather, money that paved his way.[23] Helped undeniably by the chaos in the wake of the country's total defeat in the war, Tanaka had expanded his fortune with a series of remarkable successes.[24] Tanaka's fortune-making tactics and his manner of spending money have been regarded by many as so questionable on moral as well as legal grounds that he was once described as walking on the fence that divided a prison yard from the outside world (Kodama 1974, 150). It should be pointed out here that, as Tachibana's (1974, 1976) meticulous investigative reports suggest, every politician is doing more or less the same thing. What sets Tanaka apart from the rest to such a degree is the excessive scale on which he spent and made money.

Tanaka's marriage in 1942 to the daughter of the owner of a successful construction and civil engineering company turned out to be his first big springboard toward becoming a successful businessman (Tachibana 1974, 117–18). The war had completely flattened Tokyo,

---

[23] For accounts of his early years, see Tanaka (1972, 1973); Inoue (1976); along with Togawa (1980, 38–39, 104–5); and Miyagi (1982).

[24] For details on this point, see Tachibana (1974, 117–31; 1976, vol. 1).

and construction works were in enormous demand. His fast-expanding company soon was included in the list of Japan's top fifty civil engineering and construction enterprises. His financial power attracted politicians who in the period of political anomie tried to establish a new party. They asked Tanaka for a three-million yen political donation, which was worth more than 300 million yen at today's value.[25] This incident introduced the political world to him. The newly established Shinpotō (Progressive party) invited Tanaka, then age twenty-seven, to run for a seat in the first postwar general election in April 1946.

The first election illuminates succinctly that Tanaka had a proclivity toward embodying liminality; that is, he was a deformer who tried hard to push himself to the center of the system, not by taking the well-traveled steps upward but, instead, by exploiting the system's fragile or soft part, the interstices of established structures. By paying little respect to existing institutional arrangements, he tried to use money to overpower and invalidate the established cultural and political rules and customs of the constituency in order to win the election. At the beginning of the election campaign, Tanaka gave each of a number of local influentials in Niigata an unusually large amount of cash, ranging from 100 thousand to 200 thousand yen (today equal to 10 to 20 million yen) to collect votes for him (Tachibana 1974, 119). A youthful twenty-seven-year-old Tanaka appeared before the people of the war-torn country wearing a pretentious mustache and a cutaway coat (Kodama 1974, 148). Although he was proud and confident, local influentials ridiculed and cheated him. Some of them decided to run for election themselves by using the very money he had given them. On this first try, Tanaka lost the election (Tachibana 1974, 118–19; Jyōhō Kenkyūsho 1983, 24).

On his second try, he, in addition to money, made full use of his own people, that is, his extended family members and old acquaintances from his village (Tachibana 1974; Tachibana 1976, vol. 1). All of Tanaka's political and business organizations[26] consist of these people and thus are able to be independent of or, to put it the other way around, excluded from the world of the establishment. Tanaka's most trusted "right-hand man" was a former barmaid and divorcée. She came from a poor family in the region of Niigata where Tanaka was born and has long been regarded by him as his "family member" (*miuchi*) (Kodama 1974, 145). Almost all the political money, which

---

[25] Tachibana (1974, 116): $1 = 308 yen at the time Tachibana was writing this investigative report.

[26] See a concise schematization of them in Tachibana (1974, 118, 120, 124).

was estimated in 1974 to be at least two billion yen, both legal and illegal, of Tanaka's faction and other political organizations over which he presided—came and went under her control. Despite her shadowy existence in the formal world, therefore, she held an enormous influence among politicians and businessmen who came to rely on Tanaka's political and financial power. The successful, and sometimes legally questionable, business practices of Takana's core politico-business organizations produced huge amounts of money.[27]

Tanaka spent money excessively for political purposes. For example, not only members of the Tanaka faction and other LDP factions but also the opposition members received huge sums of money from Tanaka's political organizations. Tachibana's lists show that the amount ranged from one million to about 155 million yen per person during the period between 1971 and the first half of 1973. The total number of individual LDP Diet members who received more than one million yen in that period was sixty-one. In addition to individuals, various political organizations and opposition parties were believed to receive money from Tanaka (Tachibana 1974, 108–11). This money—formally recorded under "research expenses," "organizational activities' expenses," or "political donations"—was said to be only the tip of the iceberg.

Politicians were not the lone beneficiaries. Bureaucrats, too, were given unprecedentedly expensive gifts or hard cash at occasions, such as the traditional twice-a-year gift-giving seasons, in the summer and at year's end. One ranking bureaucrat of the Finance Ministry said that since Tanaka became Finance Minister in 1962, officials of that ministry started receiving several hundred thousand yen in cash during the gift-giving seasons (until 1970, the exchange rate was fixed at $1 = 360 yen). This was deemed outrageous not only because the amount was 50 to 100 times as much as they had received from Tanaka's predecessors but also because some of the gifts were in hard cash. In Japan, cash as a gift is often considered inappropriate and distasteful or even revolting. These bureaucrats used to receive such gifts as fabrics for their wives or a box of assorted hams, fruits, or soap for their families.[28]

By the time Tanaka's faction head, Satō Eisaku, decided to step down from the prime minister's post in 1972 to be succeeded by his

[27] For investigative reports on Tanaka's "tricky" business practices, which put him at the center of the rumors of political corruption several times, see Tachibana (1974; Tachibana 1976, vol. 1).

[28] Ishihara (1974, 103). For the Japanese custom of gift-exchange, see Befu (1967) and Ohnuki-Tierney (1984, 203–6, 217–18).

favorite, the "Crown Prince," elite bureaucrat-turned-politician Fukuda Takeo, Tanaka's politico-financial power enabled him to challenge this tacit, taken-for-granted line of succession. Legitimate succession by lineage, from "King" Satō to "Crown Prince" Fukuda,
never took place. Tanaka wrested the post of prime minister by col-
lecting more votes than Fukuda in the party election.[29] To win as
many votes as possible, Tanaka was said to have spent some 3 to 5
billion yen (Tachibana 1974, 91).

All this should not be interpreted simplistically that Tanaka bought
votes or that transactions based on a cost-benefit calculation were involved. Neither money nor personality alone would make a person
one of the most popular prime ministers. As countless books and
articles on and about Tanaka clearly suggest, Tanaka's peculiar at-
tractiveness to his fellow politicians and to the general public did not
derive solely from the power of his money or from his personality.[30]

Analyzed in our theoretical framework, Tanaka's excessive spending can be seen as deforming taken-for-granted institutional arrangements. Had Tanaka never existed, "Crown Prince" Fukuda would have
succeeded Satō according to the tacitly established rules of succession. Fukuda, a former elite bureaucrat, was in every respect a qual-
ified successor with his academic background, personal ties within
the politico-bureaucratic world, and financial networks in business
circles. To those members of the LDP who did not share such qualifications with Fukuda, Tanaka's excessive spending to beat Fukuda
may have appeared intriguingly attractive.

By spending cash excessively, Tanaka relativized the taken-for-
granted rules. That is, a previously undoubted practice lost its
exclusive legitimacy. In comparison with Fukuda, Tanaka had an un-
questionably more attractive personality, outgoing, magnanimous,
talkative, and warm-hearted, plus a blasting vitality and energy that
aroused excitement among people. Younger members of the party
who wanted generational change sooner in the leadership were
drawn to Tanaka in his efforts to negate the established rules of succession. And thanks to Tanaka, such rules came to appear to them as
only arbitrary. Tanaka invalidated a legitimate "Crown Prince" by exposing his deficiency in a new set of qualifications. In so doing, Tanaka's deformative function permitted fluidity at the center of the
structures, thereby allowing for the possibility of self-regeneration
even from within the core of nomos.

[29] For a detailed account of this period, see Togawa (1980–81, vol. 3).
[30] On this point, see the argument in chap. 2, sec. 2.

Nakasone Yasuhiro

Unlike Tanaka, Nakagawa, and the Seirankai members, Nakasone Yasuhiro's early years were those of a very promising elite. He was born in 1918 to a wealthy timber dealer in a city near Tokyo. From the beginning, Nakasone was a well-disciplined, well-mannered, good-looking, and very smart boy.[31] Upon graduation from the law school of the Imperial University of Tokyo, he entered the bureaucratic world. Had war not broken out, Nakasone might well have escalated himself to the top bureaucratic post, as many observers then and now assumed (Togawa 1980–1981, 4:249; Saitō 1983, 28). Nakasone became an official of the Home Affairs Ministry in 1941 when war was escalating. After only one week's work as an elite bureaucrat, Nakasone joined the navy. He survived the war physically, but the devastating defeat of his country, which he had witnessed with his own eyes, including, from afar, the drop of an atomic bomb on Hiroshima, did affect his mentality. Pursuing individual success as an elite bureaucrat appeared meaningless to him.[32] Nakasone left the bureaucratic world in 1946 to become a politician.

A brief look at Nakasone's prepolitician years gives the impression that by no means could he embody liminal qualities. The only possibility that he could might be the result of the catastrophic era he went through. Great catastrophe did, indeed, have a significant effect on people's mentality, as much as it had upon their physical conditions. During a great catastrophe or crisis, various new religious movements, perceptions, heroes, and attitudes emerge. History shows a number of such examples, including Joan of Arc in France during the Hundred Years' War with Britain, the dozens of former housewives and former misfits of new religious movements during the chaotic civil war period spanning the last phase of the Edo and the dawn of the Meiji periods in Japan, or hippies during the Vietnam War. As V. Turner (1977, chap. 4, 148) suggests, the experience of such a chaotic liminal era would induce a reorganization of the component elements of the old order under a new principle, while also incorporating new elements. That is, it is not that the liminal, chaotic time produces a leader of marginal nature; rather, in a liminal period, ordinary people's cosmos is affected so that their mentality becomes more receptive to new views and values that are drastically different from existing ones. In other words, an era of chaos or liminality is

---

[31] For biographical accounts of Nakasone, see Suzuki (1976); Jinbo (1978); Togawa (1980–81, 4:246–54); Ajīru Kōbō (1983); and Saitō (1983).

[32] Jinbo (1978, 103–5); Togawa (1980–81, 4:248–49); and Ajīru Kōbō (1983, 124, 146–47).

the period when an extraordinary fluidity of nomos will allow possibilities that new kinds of qualities, values, and symbols may become salient.

The liminal era contributed to the transformation of Nakasone from a serious, straightforward member of the elite who could have been a core bearer of the existing order into a challenger to authority—in this case, that of the Supreme Command of the Allied Powers (SCAP), which occupied Japan for seven years until 1952, and the Japanese government, which operated under the SCAP. Nakasone's famous extreme actions and behavior, therefore, were seen chiefly during the occupation years.

As a challenger, Nakasone naturally joined the opposition camp in 1947. From the very beginning, Nakasone's radicalism on and off the Diet floor surprised people, angered authorities, and stirred controversies. For example, throughout the occupation period, Nakasone wore a black tie, insisting that he was in mourning for his country, which was in a death state until it was set free from foreign occupation (Jinbo 1978, 106; Ajiru Kōbō 1983, 32, 34). On the Diet floor, the freshman politician Nakasone was frequently the center of attention. He was a distinctly harsh critic of Prime Minister Yoshida Shigeru's policies. Actually, those attacks were directed toward the SCAP's occupation policies. Soon he earned two popular nicknames: "*Hiodoshi no yoroi o kita wakamusha*" (youthful samurai in a pristine suit of armor sewn with red thread) and "*Seinen shōkō*" (young military officer) (Jinbo 1978, 109; Togawa 1980–81, 4:253–54; Ajiru Kōbō 1983, 25, 35).

Recklessness, severity, and unpredictability were mixed with purity, innocence, and sincerity in the youthful politician Nakasone. His nicknames captured these traits. More than that, these nicknames intuitively reflected an anachronistic out-of-place quality in Nakasone's actions and behavior: a samurai, warrior of the Middle Ages in a modern political world; one of those radical prewar military officers, who were responsible for a series of assassinations of the top leaders of the country, a prewar radical in a postwar American-style Diet.

A noble samurai in the Middle Ages and a young military officer of prewar Japan are two of the most articulate embodiments of the deep-rooted indigenous Japanese spiritualism. And that is precisely the chief target the SCAP wanted to invalidate in order to fill the Japanese with American democratic ideals. Under the SCAP ordinance, every trait of traditional Japanese values were extinguished from family, school, public office, business, media, and even the art world. In short, Nakasone embodied what was forbidden by the new authority, that is, forbidden to exist in an American-imposed nomos.

Nakasone committed a series of political extremes against particular policies of the SCAP and its authority in general. His radical deeds included the 1951 *"Hinomaru nōmin demo"* (Peasants' and Farmers' Rising-Sun Demonstration), which he organized and led to protest the government's introduction of a sweeping tax system under U.S. guidance. Every one of the several hundreds of participants wore a Rising-Sun headband, and some carried a coffin to which was attached the name of the taxation office director (Jinbo 1978, 108–9; Ajīru Kōbō 1983, 34; Saitō 1983, 32). A former news reporter who was there recalled that the demonstration looked strangely uncanny (Ajīru Kōbō 1983, 34).

In late January 1951, Nakasone went to the SCAP headquarters to submit his written opinions and criticisms of the policies of the Occupation Army under General MacArthur. His requests included the earliest possible independence and the reestablishment of Japan's own defense system (Jinbo 1978, 109–11; Saitō 1983, 33–36). According to a former American officer at the MacArthur headquarters, Nakasone's paper of some sixty pages outraged MacArthur so much that the American ripped it and threw it into the trash at once.[33] Seen in the context of the time, Nakasone's deed was breathtakingly reckless. At that time, General MacArthur was such an absolute entity that even the Japanese emperor was considered to be in no position to criticize his authority and policies (Jinbo 1978, 111). Already, the Japanese had been greatly shocked by a picture in which the emperor in a formal cutaway coat stood—not sat—beside General MacArthur, who was in shirtsleeves with his arms akimbo. As that picture eloquently told the Japanese people, the authority of General MacArthur, commander-in-chief of the SCAP, was nearly impossible to attack openly.

In both cases, Nakasone defied SCAP authority outright. He directly countered American democratic ideals with an indigenous Japanese value by having all peasant demonstrators wear the Rising-Sun headband; by sending a death sentence to the Japanese who collaborated with the foreign authorities; and by refusing to be imbued in any way with alien values under alien rule by force.

Nakasone had been pursuing what was forbidden to exist and what was forced to be forgotten. He may not have been a marginal politician by nature. But, the era of chaos in the wake of the country's fatal defeat seemed to help create conditions in which behavior and actions of even a potential core elitist like Nakasone came to embody liminal qualities. These qualities consisted of the ordinary people's

[33] Jinbo (1978, 110); *Sankei Shimbun*, Dec. 13, 1975.

unshaped, unseen longings that were at the outer margin of nomos. Nakasone, at the time of great fluidity, found himself fit to blur boundaries of realities and illusions in order to relativize the nomos-based, seemingly absolute authority of the foreign occupation power. That might explain why despite Japanese government and SCAP dismay, annoyance, and, sometimes, fury, Nakasone's extremes were perceived with much sympathy and, often, enthusiastic cheers by the Japanese people and the members of the opposition.[34] Indeed, the view that sees in Nakasone during the occupation period a prototype of Japan's anachronistic popular hero is not unique.[35]

What should be of utmost significance in Nakasone's extremes is that they offered the Japanese people an opportunity to peek into other realities that were forbidden or not materialized and, in so doing, to reflect upon their present states of being. If Nakasone's challenges to the absolute authority of the SCAP did not result in much success in nomos, they are by no means simply meaningless, foolish deeds committed by an attention-hungry man, as some critical observers think (Ajīru Kōbō 1983, 34–37). The anachronistic, out-of-place hero who challenged the impossible in vain may have succeeded in mediating between nomos and chaos or between nomos and cosmos by blurring border lines of nomos with his extremes.

[34] This point is well acknowledged by many observers including Chūma (1983, 126); and Saitō (1983, 31).

[35] See, for example, Chūma (1983, 126).

Chapter Five

CONCLUSION: ON THE BASIS FOR DEMOCRACY AND SOCIAL TRANSFORMATION

THE DEREIFYING EFFECT OF PEOPLE'S REFLEXIVITY

T HE CASE STUDIES presented in the preceding chapters on various forms of marginal beings and liminal states—ranging from politicians in whom liminal qualities were embodied, an orgiastic election campaign, and a blood oath ritual to tears, comedians, and play—support the argument developed in chapter 1. I introduced several scholars of different disciplines who have presented analyses of various marginal beings and liminal states to indicate that their function is to relativize, level, and pose questions to anything in nomos, and, in so doing, to activate people's reflexivity.

As analyzed in each chapter's discussion section, the examples of marginal beings and liminal states studied in this volume are congruent with the view that they are deformers of the context and thereby allow the possibility of transformation. Because they inherently embody two or more mutually incompatible or even contradictory sets of values and principles, marginal beings and liminal states, even their mere presence inevitably brings inconsistencies and ambiguities into ordinary people's lives in nomos. As a consequence, the classification of matters and people loses its clarity, boundaries among roles and statuses are blurred, and institutional arrangements may appear arbitrary. Given this dereifying effect brought in by the marginal beings and liminal states, people's reflexivity would be activated. They would feel an urgent need to restore consistency and meaningfulness to their daily lives in nomos. This operation necessarily involves a higher level of people's worldview, that is, cosmos, as Terrence Turner (1977) so analyzes.

In the case studies, we have seen that the Finance Committee members, a candidate and the people of his constituency, and Nakasone and the rest of the LDP Executive Board members, have all experienced moments of becoming marginal beings or entering liminal states. In these experiences, they were thrown into the world of inconsistencies and ambiguities owing to the dereifying function of the liminal. Members of the LDP and the opposition in the Finance Committee, for instance, slighted the existing formal rules and regulations as well as political roles that the two camps were expected to play. This was not because they intentionally ignored them based on a cost-benefit calculation; rather, it was because intrusions of liminal states and their deformative function made existing institutional arrangements in nomos appear invalidated, arbitrary, or at least lacking in exclusive legitimacy.

The same can be said of Watanuki and his constituents and Nakasone and the executive board members. Differences among statuses, definitions of roles, and classifications of people as well as matters were blurred. Values and principles were relativized. Consequently, they had an opportunity to reflect upon themselves, that is, their analysis of themselves, their relationships with others, and the institutional arrangements of the whole system to which they belonged. This activated reflexivity enabled them to resist a reifying force of any kind. In other words, to them Diet laws no longer appeared to have absolute value. The same was true of Tanaka and his colleague supporters. To them, tacitly taken-for-granted rules of succession of the Liberal Democratic party came to look irrelevant. Reflexivity made anything appear subject to questioning. People could thus be permitted to modify views and definitions of anything, including themselves.

We have also learned from our analyses in chapter 3, that the seemingly trivial daily behavior and activities of ordinary people, such as playing, laughing, and shedding tears, have the same significant effect on ordinary people's reflexivity. Even though each of such liminal states seems insignificant at first thought, a myriad of them—ubiquitously found in our daily lives—may together exert a vast energy to ceaselessly question the existing order and institutional arrangements.

It may, then, be formulated that these metaphoric marginal beings and liminal states are the potential agents of transformation. They have this potential without any conscious intention, objective, or strategy. No matter what political, economic, cultural, or historical system they belong to, marginal beings and liminal states ranging from laughter, daydreams, and critical illness to war, millenarian movements, and natural catastrophe fit this formulation. This potential is precisely the reason why Marcuse (1978)[1] sees in romanticist and symbolist poems such as those of Boudelaire, or in surrealist

---

[1] See also Marcuse (1969, 1972).

paintings—rather than, for example, the proletarian art and literature created intentionally to liberate—a genuine force for ultimate human emancipation in this modern "one-dimensional" society.

We can now argue that the potential of marginal beings and liminal states to bring about genuine, three-dimensional social change is the power of neutralizing any form of reifying force. Or, we may say that the marginal beings and liminal states are the answer to the problem of false consciousness (Marxist terminology for reified consciousness), and neither class struggle nor education nor consciousness-raising effort by the party and/or intellectuals is the answer. These neutralizers operate exclusively within the sphere of symbolic margin and interstices where the unconscious, metaphoric, symbolic, aesthetic, and spontaneous human dimension overpowers norm-governed, utilitarian, that is, metonymic activities. Their operation in neutralizing the reifying force is accomplished by keeping people's reflexivity activated. Reflexivity allows ordinary people to be always available to reexamine realities, including themselves, and to bend on their interpretive processes. Reflexivity, furthermore, belongs to the unconscious, symbolic dimension, and hence has nothing to do with conscious learning or purposeful education from outside.

Raising people's political consciousness is a task that should take place in the dimension of consciousness, order, and praxis, that is, nomos. In a word, an argument on whether political consciousness is *high* or *low* is not always meaningful. As we have seen, individuals' very basic consciousnesses, such as who they are, what they are, what their rights are, what they want, and so forth, can be structured and reified in a certain way. That is, individuals are by no means masters of their own consciousnesses. It is, therefore, often irrelevant to speak simplistically of the level of political consciousness as an index of democracy. "High political consciousness" could mean merely a highly structured and reified consciousness. Individuals of such consciousness cannot really reflect themselves into the political process. They reflect their structured and reified consciousnesses, that is, false consciousness as the Marxist scholars call it. In such circumstances, any *democratic* political arrangements, for example, one-man-one-vote and direct participation in the decision-making process, will do little.

The marginal beings and liminal states do not convey democratic ideology nor do they, in one way or another, democratically educate people. Quite apart from that, they evoke people's active, voluntary, and creative participation *in the process* of politics by ceaselessly preventing people's reflexivity from being suppressed and, thereby, helping liberate reified consciousness. With only those people whose consciousness is kept from being fully structured and reified (owing to their activated reflexivity) could democratic political arrangements in nomos have some meaning.

Still, the main issue to be clarified in this study is how marginal beings and liminal states could allow the possibility of three-dimensional change.[2] It is crucial for us to dissect the structure of change and then to offer a logical explanation. Obviously, to shake the legitimacy of the existing authority or value system is not the same as to bring about genuine, three-dimensional change, although it is certainly possible to assume that the shaken legitimacy might lead to a change eventually. What is lacking here, however, is the clarification of the structure of change.

Let us begin with a schematization of the three-dimensional world-view as suggested by Berger (1969) and refined by Ueno (1977).

| COSMOS |
| NOMOS |
| CHAOS |

Theoretically, genuine change could take place in three ways:

1. Increase of CHAOS —→ disintegration of NOMOS —→ modification of COSMOS. In this case, that is, CHAOS —→ NOMOS —→ COSMOS, the nature or constitution of the end result is least sure.

2. Reorganization in NOMOS —→ modification or even total reconstruction of COSMOS and change in CHAOS. This version, that is, NOMOS —→ COSMOS —→ CHAOS is adopted by the Marxist orthodoxy[3] as well as by modern social science scholars, and practitioners alike.

3. Modification in COSMOS —→ reorganization in NOMOS —→ change in CHAOS. Those who take this view, that is, COSMOS —→ NOMOS —→ CHAOS have been and are treated significantly

[2] Incidentally, the view that equates social changes with the redistribution of social resources, that is, a reshuffling within nomos, is commonly held by many social scientists, such as Meyer (1972, chap. 11) and Tominaga (1965, 253; Tominaga 1973).

[3] Significantly, Marx in his early years did not rely on this version; see, for example, Marx (1964, 61–219) "Economic and Philosophical Manuscripts 1844."

unfairly by being called *utopians* or are otherwise regarded as religious believers rather than serious thinkers or practitioners of the real world.[4]

These three models of change suggested by Ueno (1977) are very useful in clarifying the structures of three-dimensional change. Still, these models are unable to see ordinary people's daily behavior and activities—that is, ordinary people's experiences of moments of liminal states as well as embodiments of liminal qualities—as deformers and thus potential agents of transformation. We have already introduced in chapter 1 our modified scheme of worldview that consists not only of cosmos, nomos, and chaos but also of the marginal/liminal domains between each of them.[5]

The significance of the insertion of the liminal domains between cosmos and nomos and between chaos and nomos now should be made clear. The insertion permits us to come to a new concept that holds that ordinary people's daily behavior and activities are the crucial agents of changes. Moreover, we can realize that without liminal domains between each of the three dimensions, the occurrences in one dimension may not be automatically related to other dimensions. In this sense, therefore, the Berger-Ueno model is not satisfactorily persuasive because it does not offer a logical explanation for why an increase in chaos, for example, can and needs to affect cosmos and nomos. That is, if we assume that clear demarcation lines exist—rather than mediating domains of marginal beings and liminal states—between each of the three dimensions, a conceivable, more natural course that follows the occurrences in one dimension is a strengthening of defense mechanisms, instead of self-adjustment on the part of other dimensions, except for those cases in which such occurrences are of extraordinary magnitude.

As we have examined throughout this book, however, three dimensions are casually being mediated by a wide variety of marginal beings and liminal states. Because of the existence of the liminal domains, three dimensions are kept available for influencing and modifying one another. Owing to the mediation of the liminal domains, in other words, reifying force is constantly disturbed. Nomos is exposed to the ubiquitous and ceaseless intrusions from both chaos and

---

[4] In this respect, see Wolff and Moore (1967); Engels (1968) and critiques of Marcuse by Breines (1970); Aronson (1971); Breines (1971), Jay (1971), and Inagami (1974, 315–17).

[5] More precisely, the nomos domain should be drawn like a fishing net to indicate that liminality breaks in through the interstices.

cosmos. The intrusions cause inconsistencies and ambiguities in nomos. They are deformers and relativizers.

As Leach (1961b, 1976) maintains, it is not chaos alone that contradicts nomos. Cosmos, too, rests on the organizational principle that contrasts that of nomos.[6] Inevitably, therefore, all marginal beings and liminal states, whether they embody cosmos-nomos or nomos-chaos elements, bring about inconsistencies and ambiguities in nomos. In their experiences of liminal moments, ordinary people could reach cosmos, where, to use V. Turner's (1968, 577) terms, people could return to a first principle of culture to be aware of the possibilities of any and every recombination of elements. These reflexive processes might allow for the possibility of modification in cosmos. That in turn might lead to the transformation of the society because cosmos is constituted by the most fundamental, abstract ideas and values that determine the type and scope of interpretations and views in nomos. Modification in cosmos, in short, would induce change of the basic organizational principle of the component elements of nomos.

To be sure, the transformation we are talking about here has absolutely no positive or negative connotation. Marginal beings and liminal states never advocate or embody certain consistent values nor do they set objectives. The change they could bring about, however, is by no means peripheral. The significance of this change is that it continues to help regenerate ordinary people's worldviews and, hence, the social context of which they are a part. It rejuvenates people's reflexivity and sharpens their senses. It is not brought about by conscious, intentional plan or activities.

Too often, a spontaneous, elemental outburst by ordinary people, for example, is viewed negatively by scholars and revolutionaries such as Trotsky (1969, 99) and Fanon (1966, 45–46). The latter contemplates that through ecstatic collective activities, such as dancing at carnival, people's energy that should be directed toward and used for the mass struggle for liberation is "canalized, transformed, and conjured away" (Fanon 1966, 45). Nevertheless, if people are deprived of such spontaneous self-expressions and liminal, aesthetic experiences and instead are filled with the teachings of revolutionary ideology and practical strategies for the attainment of certain goals, their symbolic, metaphoric, liminal dimension will be suppressed. Forced to think and live only within the domain of nomos, people's

---

[6] Although mutual compatibility and a hierarchical relationship between cosmos and nomos are popularly contemplated in sociology (e.g., Berger and Luckmann [1966]; Berger [1969]), the independent, ontological, and irreducible quality of cosmos may well contradict nomos principles, as Durkheim (1965) suggested.

reflexivity would wane. The result, naturally, is that they would be reduced to nothing more than masses of reified (or false) consciousness, an easy and willing prey for domination.

No matter what kind of marginal being or liminal state it may be, whether it is ecstatic dancing, play, fantasy, critical illness, or war, it is an agent that keeps ordinary people from being reified. Being reflexive, not totally reified, is indispensable for any individual to maintain genuine freedom—that is, freedom to think, see, and act with greater independence from any form of domination—and, hence, maintain power as well. Democracy should consist of this kind of people, people with an activated reflexivity. Democratic political arrangements, such as direct participation in the decision-making process, could be little different from outright totalitarianism if the people's consciousness is completely reified.

FREEDOM, DEMOCRACY, AND INDIVIDUALISM

Our discussion in the introductory chapter led us to a new concept of power as well as society and its dynamics. No one in society can be completely free from being reified with a certain worldview at any time. Reification progresses and deepens through various kinds of mechanisms that are built into the numerous cultural institutions of the society. As we have learned from Foucault, Gramsci, Althusser, and the poststructuralists, reifying force is working largely anonymously and ubiquitously without letting people become aware of it.

To an individual, then, freedom and power must mean how well each can neutralize the force of reification, if not completely. At the very basis of individual freedom and power must exist the person's least reified consciousness, a richly reflexive consciousness. Without that, any social, political, or economic arrangements might well work against the individual, at least in the long run. Some may hastily think that the more an individual and, to some extent, the society as well experience moments of becoming a marginal being and entering a liminal state, the freer and more powerful the person can be. Yet, we should keep in mind that if the marginal beings and liminal states let ambiguities and inconsistencies intrude excessively into nomos, the very existence of an individual and society itself would be in danger in the state of excessive fluidity. Neither an individual nor the society can live with fragmented pieces of worldview.

Because reifying force is working ubiquitously and anonymously at a micro level, counterforce, too, can be working most effectively at a micro level. Or, to put it differently, because the form of domination in modern times is no longer systematic or one-dimensional, as Foucault so persuasively shows, an effective form of resistance cannot be systematic or have certain identifiable targets, either. Instead of massive class struggles or organized nationwide antigovernment movements, for example, our alternative concept of power and freedom suggests paying serious attention to the seemingly insignificant, nonpolitical behavior and activities of ordinary people in their daily lives. Of particular interest should be ordinary people's potential and liability to become marginal beings and to enter liminal states. The function marginal beings and liminal states have and the kind of change they can bring about should be our chief concerns whenever we think of power and freedom at the deepest level.

Marx (1964, 1–40) in his early years had already discerned the difference between "political emancipation" and "human emancipation." The former means only the "emancipation *within* [my emphasis] the framework of the prevailing social order" (Marx 1964, 15), whereas the latter assumes a totally new social order in which man is liberated from the state of alienation. Marx (1964, 10–11) noted, "the *state* can liberate itself from a constraint without man himself being *really* liberated. . . . A state may be a *free state* without man himself being a *free man*" [Marx's emphases]. Political freedom and power are only those within the existing order. Genuine or, as Marx said, human freedom and power can be scarcely realized through "political emancipation," that is, in our terms, changes in nomos alone.

Genuine human freedom and social change, in other words, should accompany three-dimensional, cosmos-nomos-chaos change, rather than simply the rearrangements in nomos. V. Turner's conceptualization of social dynamics is very suggestive in this regard. He contemplates (V. Turner 1974: Preface) that societas—which is a holistic society consisting of *structure* and *communitas*—does not advance in a linear, continuous, sequential manner. Rather, he argues, it is disrupted with numerous intrusions of liminal phases that bend or discontinue the preceding process. Turner (1974, 14) is thus convinced that a given culture at a certain time may be thought of as a collage comprising disparate pieces of past ideologies, values, and so forth. Leach (1961a, 1961b, Leach 1976, 77–79, 33–36) offers a very clear explanation of how liminal, symbolic time and space—that is, "no man's time" (Leach 1976, 34) and space—is inserted in the ordinary flow of time, and changes the quality of it. That is, here again, we see a concept of discontinuous, nonsequential social process.[7]

---

[7] On this point, see also Lévi-Strauss' (1966, 245–69) criticism of Sartre.

Foucault (1972) criticized the linear, evolutionary perspective of history. Instead of accepting the prevailing historical stages theory of society—for example, from feudalism to capitalism to socialism—he was interested in capturing a *structure* of each period of a given society by paying meticulous attention to seemingly insignificant daily particularities. He conceived of each period as different and discontinuous from the other rather than in an evolutionary sequence. A new French school of history is basically in line with Foucault. For example, Braudel's (1980) interest is not limited to just social and economic changes. He also takes into account science, technology, ecology, climate, civilization, and the mentality of the people. He contemplates that a given society changes relatively gradually—that is, for a certain period, a society rests on structure, *A* (in structuralists' sense of the term) and after it has collapsed, a new structure, *B* becomes dominant.

In short, in his thought, just like Kuhn's (1970) "structure of the scientific revolutions," social dynamics is seen as a cyclical displacement of basic structures. Naturally, political revolution or change in the economic system alone is not regarded as significant as the more basic structural change that involves, among other things, changes in people's mentality. In Japan, too, a similar approach is employed by students of the new school of social history and culture led by Abe (1974, 1981), Amino (1978, 1980), and Amino and Abe (1982), who are equally aware of the importance of attention to trivial daily particularities in theoretical work.

What all of these scholars have in common is the notion that social dynamics involves catastrophes, large and small, in which all three dimensions, cosmos, nomos, and chaos, are inevitably the subjects to change. We would argue further that ordinary people's daily lives consist of a series of little catastrophes, and so does social process, owing to the mediation by the ubiquitous marginal beings and liminal states. Because of that, people can keep themselves from being totally reified with their present states of being. This condition is indispensable for the genuine freedom and power of ordinary people and for democracy in society as well.

Thus, it may be logically argued that democracy is not necessarily a political form that accompanies a certain historical and/or industrial level. Indeed, beyond modern Western democracy, spatially and temporally, we find a number of societies that operate on democratic principles. They include the eighteenth-century illiterate society of Dahomey (Polanyi 1966), present-day rural Nigerian communities (Weller 1986), and the Middle Ages in Japan.[8] We may also cast doubt

---

[8] Yokoi (1975); Amino (1978, 1980); Amino and Abe (1982). See also Kida (1953, 1957,

on the popular belief that Western individualism and democracy are inseparable as seen clearly in one of the most widely read works on democracy, that of Alexis de Tocqueville (1955). Not only would we be suspicious about the evolutionary perspective that regards individualism as an advanced form of industrial/postindustrial societies[9] but we also should question more fundamentally individualism itself.

Foucault's works on power (1978, 1979a, 1979b, 1980, 1981, 1983) indicate that individualization of each subject, that is, *assujettissement* (submission of subjectivity) is very likely related to Christianity. What Foucault calls the "pastoral power" accompanied Christianity in Europe in the Middle Ages, induced an individual to turn himself into an individualized subject, and took new forms in modern states. The fact, as Foucault points out, that in modern Western societies this type of individualizing tactic of pastoral power found support in enormously varied kinds of cultural institutions suggests that basically Christianity does seem to be working for the reinforcement as well as dissemination of this peculiar form of individuality. Outside the Christian-oriented cultural tradition, this type of individuality might be nonexistent. Although it may be too extreme to say that Western individualism is a product of Christianity, it can be at least suggested that Western individualism is only one form of individuality that is closely related to Christianity.

It then appears irrelevant to identify Western individualism as a sole, universal kind, and, hence, to regard different forms of individuality in other non-Christian societies as "collectivism" (i.e., a deficiency in individuality), adding the connotation of a less advanced stage of development. The Japanese have been regarded as being unaware of, or at the less-developed stage of, individualism.[10] More recently, some observers of Japan and the Japanese began arguing, while cautioning against using only one standard for comparison, that the Japanese are as individualistic as Westerners (Mouer and Sugimoto 1986, chap. 8). Still, they do not go far enough in dissociating Judeo-Christian–oriented individualism from democracy. In other words, generally, recent scholars who try to explore the "individualistic" aspects of the Japanese[11] tend to argue that the Japanese

1967, 1981) and Irokawa (1975) for the descriptions of democratic egalitarianism observed in Japanese rural communities from the premodern era through, during, and after World War II.

[9] See Parsons (1951).

[10] See, for example, Nakane (1970); DeVos (1973, chaps. 7, 14; DeVos 1975); and Nakamura (1974).

[11] Oda, (1969); Krauss, Rohlen, and Steinhoff (1984); and Mouer and Sugimoto (1986, especially 191–210).

are, or *are becoming*, as individualistic as Westerners are. Therefore, they surmise Japanese are, or are becoming, liberated or democratic; or the Japanese, "given" the democratic ideology after the defeat in World War II, have become aware of individualism.

In general, when scholars argue about whether a given society rests upon individualism or collectivism, they are basing their argument on the same static view of society and the individual. That is, as Asada (1986, 132–45) cogently argues, a society is popularly conceptualized as a self-contained network of relations. In such a case, if one emphasizes the entire network, one tends to see a society of collectivism, whereas if one pays major attention to each grid of the network of relations, one may well get a society that consists of atoms, that is, a society of individualism. Either way, society is viewed as a static, self-contained entity.

We have explored in this book, however, the theory that the networks of relations in a society are in constant movement and intertwined with one another in many layers. We may, therefore, in line with Asada (1986, 141), conceive of each individual in a society as an ever-shifting (shrinking, expanding, and changing places) bundle of communication lines—communication in its broadest sense, embracing physical and spiritual exchanges with others and the outside world. As neither an atom nor a barely recognizable part of the whole an individual now appears as an evasive body of multiple social relations that is infinitely open to a wide range of physical and cultural contacts with others. In short, the existing notions of individualism, collectivism, and totalitarianism are, after all, not much different from one another. In all of them it is presupposed that individuals are atoms within a self-contained network of relations. The difference lies in where one puts prior emphasis: on atoms (individualism), networks (relationism), or a whole (holism/collectivism).

The point is that individualism is not the opposite of collectivism or relationism. To try to contrast these three types of state of being does not seem to be meaningful. Neither is it worthwhile to try to associate one particular type with a particular kind of political system, such as individualism with democracy. Moreover, as we have seen, the ability of self-expression or level of political consciousness cannot be comfortably associated with democracy either. Even completely reified individuals can express self-interest. Who they are, what they are, what they value, and so forth can be firmly determined by their worldviews if they are reified, and they can still speak out about what they want. Reified consciousness does not prevent individuals from perceiving and analyzing things, others, and themselves and expressing what they think their self-interests are. The question is not whether individuals know (or more precisely, think they know) and express their individual self-interest or not; it is, instead, how free from reification their perceptions are of their self-interest, of themselves, of others, and of society.

The argument so far has recapitulated the three major points made in this book. First, social dynamics is not constituted by linear, developmental stages but by discontinuous, sometimes even mutually incompatible phases, each of which is separated by a catastrophe, small or large. Second, power and freedom depend on how much individuals are free from reification; in other words, how reflexive their consciousness is; how well they are equipped to neutralize the reifying force; or how individuals and society as well are open to and tolerant of the marginal beings and liminal states through whose mediation both ordinary people and an entire society can continue to activate reflexivity, the counterforce to reification. And third, the most fundamental and indispensable prerequisite for democracy is neither certain political, economic institutional arrangements, nor Western individualism, which is just one of many different forms of individuality. It is the freedom of consciousness from total reification and the reflexive power of neutralizing the reifying force. The case studies in the preceding chapters illustrate these points. On the whole, they suggest the possibilities of a new kind of social dynamics concept—namely, that of discontinuous and mutually contradictory phases; the magnitude of influence the marginal beings and liminal states could exert; and a notion of democracy that does not rest on Western individualism or specific formal political and economic institutions.

REFERENCES CITED

Abe Kinya. 1974. *Hāmerun no fuefuki otoko* (A piper of Hameln). Tokyo: Heibonsha.

———. 1978. *Keiri no shakaishi* (A social history of executioners). Tokyo: Chūō Kōron.

———. 1981. *Chūsei no mado kara* (From a window of the Middle Ages). Tokyo: Asahi Shimbunsha.

Aida Nirō. 1962. *Nihon no komonsho* (Japan's old manuscripts). 2 vols. Tokyo: Iwanami Shoten.

Ajīru Kōbō, ed. 1983. *Nakasone Yasuhiro zen kenshō* (Comprehensive research on Nakasone Yasuhiro). Tokyo: Yēll Shuppansha.

Akasaka Tarō. 1983. " 'Sansaiba' Nakagawa Ichirō no kaishi" (Strange death of a "youthful horse" Nakagawa Ichirō). *Bungei Shunjū* 61(March): 300–4.

Akiyama Kōtarō. 1973. "Ketsumei shita takaha shūdan" (A hawkish group took a blood oath). *Asahi Jānaru* 15(Aug. 3): 10–12.

Almond, Gabriel A., and B. Gringham Powell, Jr. 1966. *Comparative Politics: A Developmental Approach*. Boston: Little, Brown.

Althusser, Louis, and Etienne Balibar. 1970. *Reading Capital*, trans. Ben Brewster. London: NLB; New York: Pantheon Books.

Amino Yoshihiko. 1978. *Muen, Kugai, Raku* (Muen, Kugai, and Raku). Tokyo: Heibonsha.

———. 1980. *Nihon Chūsei no minshūzō* (An image of ordinary people of the Middle Ages in Japan). Tokyo: Iwanami Shoten.

Amino Yoshihiko, and Abe Kinya. 1982. *Chūsei no saihakken* (Rediscovery of the Middle Ages). Tokyo: Heibonsha.

Aoi Kazuo. 1974. "Shakai taikei no shinsō riron" (A theory of deep social structure). In *Shakaigaku kōza* (Sociology lectures). Pp. 239–308 in vol. 1, *Riron shakaigaku* (Theoretical sociology), ed. Aoi Kazuo. Tokyo: Tokyo Daigaku Shuppankai.

Aronson, Ronald. 1971. "Dear Herbert." Pp. 257–80 in *The Revival of American Socialism*, ed. George Fischer. New York: Oxford University Press.

Asada Akira. 1983. *Kōzō to chikara* (Structure and power). Tokyo: Keisō Shobō.

———. 1986. *Tōsōron: Sukizo-kizzu no daibōken* (Running away: The adventure of schizo-kids). Tokyo: Chikuma Shobō.

Asahi Jānaru Henshūbu. 1983a. "Jimintō no chin sanken bunritsuron o warau" (Laughing at an LDP's phony theory of the division of powers). *Asahi Jānaru* (Sept. 30): 10–13.

———. 1983b. " 'Tanakasone' shinjūkōsu e no bōsō" (A blind dash towards Tanaka = Nakasone double suicide). *Asahi Jānaru* (Nov. 11): 6–8.

Asahi Shimbun Seijibu. 1985. *Tanaka shihai* (The Tanaka reign). Tokyo: Asahi Shimbunsha.

Babcock, Barbara A. 1980. "Reflexivity: Definitions and Discriminations." *Semiotica* 30(1/2): 1–14.

Babcock-Abrahams, Barbara. 1975. "A Tolerated Margin of Mess: The Trickster and His Tales Reconsidered." *Journal of the Folklore Institute* 11:147–86.

Baerwald, Hans H. 1974. *Japan's Parliament: An Introduction*. London: Cambridge University Press.

Bakhtin, Mikhail. 1984. *Rabelais and His World*, trans. Helene Iswolsky. Bloomington: Indiana University Press.

Barthes, Roland. 1982. *Empire of Signs*, trans. Richard Howard. New York: Hill and Wang.

Bastide, Roger. 1970. "Le Rire et les Courts-Circuits de la Pensée." Pp. 953–63 in vol. 2 of *Échange et communications*, ed. Pierre Maranda and Jean Pouillon. The Hague: Mouton.

Bataille, Georges. 1949. *La part maudite: Essai d'économic générale*. Paris: Éditions de Minuit.

———. 1951. "Sommes-nous la pour jouer? Ou pour être serieux?" Pt. 1. *Critique* 7(49): 512–22.

———. 1951. "Sommes-nous la pour jouer? Ou pour être serieux?" Pt. 2. *Critique* 7(51/52): 734–48.

———. 1954. *L'expérience Intérieure*. Paris: Gallimard.

———. 1957. "Emily Bronte." In *La littérature et le mal*. Paris: Gallimard.

———. 1973. *Shinpi, geijutsu, kagaku* (Mystery, art, and science), trans. Yamamoto Isao. Tokyo: Futami Shobō.

Beat Takeshi. 1986, *Tensai Takeshi no genki ga deru terebi !!* (Exciting TV with Takeshi the Genius !!). Tokyo: Nihon Terebi Hōsōmō (NTV).

Beck, Brenda E. F. 1978. "The Metaphor as a Mediator between Semantic and Analogic Modes of Thought." *Current Anthropology* 19(March): 83–88.

Befu, Harumi. 1967. "Gift-giving and Social Reciprocity in Japan, an Exploratory Statement." *France-Asie/Asia* 188:161–77.

———. 1974. "Power in Exchange: Strategy of Control and Patterns of Compliance in Japan." *Asian Profile* 2(5/6): 601–22.

Beidelman, T. O. 1980. "The Moral Imagination of the Kaguru: Some Thoughts on Tricksters, Translation and Comparative Analysis." *American Ethnologist* 7(Feb.): 27–42.

Berger, Peter L. 1963. *Invitation to Sociology: A Humanistic Perspective*. Garden City, N.Y.: Doubleday.

———. 1969. *The Social Reality of Religion*. London: Faber and Faber.

Berger, Peter L., and Thomas Luckmann. 1966. *The Social Construction of Reality: A Treatise in the Sociology of Knowledge*. New York: Anchor Books.

Berger, Peter L., and Stanley Pullberg. 1965. "Reification and the Sociological Critique of Consciousness." *History and Theory* 4(2): 196–211.

Bergson, Henri. 1956. "Laughter." Pp. 59–190 in *Comedy: An Essay on Comedy (by George Meredith) and Laughter (by Henri Bergson)*, ed. Wylie Sypher. Garden City, N.Y.: Doubleday.

Blau, Peter M. 1964. *Exchange and Power in Social Life*. New York: John Wiley and Sons.

————. 1968. "Interaction: Social Exchange." Pp. 452–58 in vol. 7 of *International Encyclopedia of the Social Sciences*, ed. David L. Sills. New York: Macmillan; Free Press.

Braudel, Fernand. 1980. *On History*, trans. Sarah Matthews. Chicago: University of Chicago Press.

Breines, Paul. 1971. "Marcuse and the New Left." Pp. 281–96 in *The Revival of American Socialism*, ed. George Fischer. New York: Oxford University Press.

————, ed. 1970. *Critical Interruptions: New Left Perspectives on Herbert Marcuse*. New York: Herder and Herder.

Brown, Harold I. 1979. *Perception, Theory and Commitment: The New Philosophy of Science*. Chicago: University of Chicago Press.

Burgess, John. 1986. "In Japan, Politics Is All in the Family." *Washington Post*, June 29, A23, A26.

Caillois, Roger. 1959. Pp. 152–62, "Play and the Sacred," and pp. 163–80, "War and the Sacred." In *Man and the Sacred*, trans. Meyer Barash. Glencoe, Ill.: Free Press.

————. 1961. *Man, Play, and Games*, trans. Meyer Barash. New York: Free Press of Glencoe.

Calder, Kent E. 1982. "Kanryo vs. Shomin: Contrasting Dynamics of Conservative Leadership in Postwar Japan." Pp. 1–28 in *Political Leadership in Contemporary Japan*, ed. Terry Edward MacDougall. Center for Japanese Studies, University of Michigan, Ann Arbor.

Chūma, Kiyofuku. 1983. "Nakasone shikan to 'Kindai no chōkoku' " (Nakasone's philosophy and 'Transcending modern'). *Chūō Kōron* 98(April): 120–31.

Clastres, Pierre. 1977. *Society Against the State: The Leaders as Servant and the Humane Uses of Power Among the Indians of the Americas*, trans. Robert Hurley. New York: Urizen Books.

Clegg, Stewart. 1975. *Power, Rule and Domination*. London: Routledge and Kegan Paul.

————. 1976. "Power, Theorizing, and Nihilism." *Theory and Society* 3(1976): 65–87.

————. 1977. "Power, Organization Theory, Marx and Critique." Pp. 21–40 in *Critical Issues in Organizations*, ed. Stewart Glegg and David Dunkerley. London: Routledge and Kegan Paul.

————. 1979. *The Theory of Power and Organization*. London: Routledge and Kegan Paul.

————. 1989. *Frameworks of Power*. Newbury Park, Calif.: Sage Publications.

Clegg, Stewart, and David Dunkerley. 1980. *Organization, Class and Control*. London: Routledge and Kegan Paul.

Cleugh, James. 1963. *Love Locked Out: An Examination of the Irresponsible Sexuality of the Middle Ages*. London: Blond.

Cohen, Abner. 1976. *Two-Dimensional Man*. Berkeley: University of California Press.

Cohn, Norman. 1961. *The Pursuit of the Millennium*. 2d ed. New York: Harper and Row.

———. 1970. "Medieval Millenarism: Its Bearing on the Comparative Study of Millenarian Movements." Pp. 31–43 in *Millennial Dreams in Action: Studies in Revolutionary Religious Movements*, ed. Sylvia Thrupp. New York: Schocken Books.

Cox, Harvey G. 1969. *The Feast of Fools: A Theological Essay on Festivity and Fantasy*. Cambridge, Mass.: Harvard University Press.

Curtis, Gerald. 1971. *Election Campaigning, Japanese Style*. New York: Columbia University Press.

Curtis, Gerald, and Ishikawa Masumi. 1984. *Doken kokka Nippon* (Japan, a country of construction contractors). Tokyo: Kōbunsha.

"Dakyōgeki no kurogo, 'Kokutaizoku'" (Experts of behind-the-scenes compromises, the Diet Policy Committee members). *Asahi Shimbun*, Sept. 11, 1983.

"Dasan to 'Kejime' no futōmei seikyoku" (An interplay between calculations and pursuit of a politically acceptable settlement complicates the political situation) 1983. *Ekomomisuto* 61 (Nov. 15): 28–34.

Davis, Natalie Z. 1975. *Society and Culture in Early Modern France*. Stanford, Calif.: Stanford University Press.

Deleuze, Gilles, and Félix Guattari. 1977. *Anti-Oedipus: Capitalism and Schizophrenia*, trans. Robert Hurley, Mark Seem, and Helen R. Lane). New York: Viking Press.

Derrida, Jacques. 1981. *Positions*, trans. Alan Baas. Chicago: University of Chicago Press.

DeVos, George A. 1973. *Socialization for Achievement: Essays on the Cultural Psychology of the Japanese*. Berkeley: University of California Press.

———. 1975. "Apprenticeship and Paternalism." Pp. 210–27 in *Modern Japanese Organizations and Decision-Making*, ed. Ezra F. Vogel. Berkeley: University of California Press.

Dore, Ronald P. 1958. *City Life in Japan: A Study of a Tokyo Ward*. Berkeley: University of California Press.

Douglas, Mary. 1966. *Purity and Danger: An Analysis of Concepts of Pollution and Taboo*. London: Routledge and Kegan Paul.

———. 1968. "The Social Control of Cognition: Some Factors in Joke Perception." *Man*, n.s. 3(Sept.): 361–76.

———. 1970. *Natural Symbols: Explorations in Cosmology*. London: Barrie and Rockliff, Cresset Press.

Dumont, Louis. 1970. *Homo Hierarachicus: The Caste System and Its Implications*, trans. Mark Sainsbury. London : Weidenfeld and Nicolson.

Durkhiem, Émile. 1964. *The Division of Labor in Society*, trans. George Simpson. New York: Free Press.

———. 1965. *The Elementary Forms of the Religious Life*, trans. Joseph Ward Swain. New York: Free Press.

Edwards, Walter. 1982. "Something Borrowed: Wedding Cakes as Symbols in Modern Japan." *American Ethnologist* 9(Nov.): 699–711.

Embree, John F. 1939. *Suye Mura: A Japanese Village*. Chicago: University of Chicago Press.

Engels, Friedrich. 1968. *Socialism: From Utopia to Science*, trans. Edward Aveling. New York: New York Labor News.

Erasmus, Desiderius. 1965. *The Praise of Folie*, trans. Sir Thomas Chaloner; ed. Clarence H. Miller. London: Oxford University Press.

Erikson, Kai T. 1966. *Wayward Puritans: A Study in the Sociology of Deviance*. New York: John Wiley and Sons.

Fanon, Frantz. 1966. *The Wretched of the Earth*, trans. Constance Farrington. New York: Grove Press.

Femia, Joseph. 1975. "Hegemony and Consciousness in the Thought of Antonio Gramsci." *Political Studies* 23(1): 29–48.

Fernandez, James W. 1972. "Persuasions and Performance: Of the Beast in Every body . . . and the Metaphors of Everyman." *Daedalus* 101(1): 39–60.

———. 1977. "The Performance of Ritual Metaphors." Pp.100–31 in *The Social Use of Metaphor: Essays on the Anthropology of Rhetoric*, ed. J. David Sapir and J. Christopher Crocker. Philadelphia: University of Pennsylvania Press.

Foucault, Michel. 1970. *The Order of Things*. London: Tavistock.

———. 1972. *The Archaeology of Knowledge*, trans. A. M. Sheridan Smith. New York: Pantheon Books.

———. 1977. *Language, Counter-Memory, Practice: Selected Essays and Interviews*, ed. with an intro. by Donald F. Bouchard; trans. Donald F. Bouchard and Sherry Simon. Ithaca, N.Y.: Cornell University Press.

———. 1978. "Politics and the Study of Discourse." *Ideology and Consciousness* 3(Spring): 7–26.

———. 1979a. *Discipline and Punish: The Birth of the Prison*, trans. Alan Sheridan. New York: Vintage Books.

———. 1979b. "Power and Norm: Notes." Pp. 59–66 in *Power, Truth, Strategy*, ed. Meagham Morris and Paul Patton. Sydney: Feral Publications.

———. 1980. *The History of Sexuality Vol.1 : An Introduction*, trans. by Robert Hurley. New York: Vintage Books.

———. 1981. *Power/Knowledge: Selected Interviews and Other Writings 1972–77*, ed. Colin Gordon; trans. Colin Gordon, Leo Marshall, John Mepham, and Kate Soper. New York: Pantheon Books.

———. 1983. "Afterword." Pp. 208–64 in Hubert L. Dreyfus and Paul Rabinow, *Michel Foucault: Beyond Structuralism and Hermeneutics*. Chicago: University of Chicago Press.

Frankenberg, Ronald. 1957. *Village on the Border: A Social Study of Religion, Politics and Football in a North Wales Community*. London: Cohen and West.

Freud, Sigmund. 1963. *Jokes and Their Relation to the Unconscious*, trans. and ed. James Strachey. New York: W. W. Norton.

"Fuan to shōryo no hoshutō" (The conservative Liberal Democratic party in anxiety and frustration). 1974. *Ekonomisuto* 52(Feb. 26): 33.

Fujiwara Hirotatsu. 1980. "Fujiwara Hirotatsu kenka taidan: Kimitachi wa dō tatakauka" (Provocatively frank talk with Fujiwara Hirotatsu: How are you going to fight to pave your way?) *Gendai* 14(Jan.): 114–34.

Fukaya Takashi. 1982. *Senkyo no senjutsu, senryaku—Seijika o mezasu hito no tameni* (Strategies and tactics to win the election—for those who are planning to be politicians). Tokyo: Jiyū Minshutō Kenshūkyoku.

Fukuoka Masayuki. 1983. "Naze tsuyoi Kakuei seiji" (Why Tanaka Kakuei's political strategies work so effectively). *Chūō Kōron* 98(1): 112–22.

Fukutake Tadashi. 1971. *Nihon no nōson* (Japanese rural community). Tokyo: Tokyo Daigaku Shuppankai.

Geertz, Clifford. 1972. "Deep Play: Notes on the Balinese Cockfight." *Daedalus* 101 (Winter): 1–37.

———. 1973. *The Interpretation of Cultures: Selected Essays*. New York: Basic Books.

Gendai Seiji Mondai Kenkyūkai, ed. 1973. *Jimintō gigokusi* (A history of the Liberal Democratic party scandals). Tokyo: Gendai Hyōronsha.

———. 1979. *Jimintō akumei retsuden* (Who's who of the notorious members of the Liberal Democratic party). Tokyo: Gendai Hyōronsha.

Gibney, Frank. 1975. *Japan: The Fragile Super Power*. Tokyo: Charles E. Tuttle.

Ginzburg, Carlo. 1982. *The Cheese and the Worms: The Cosmos of 16th Century Miller*, trans. John Tedeschi and Anne Tedeschi. New York: Penguin Books.

———. 1984. *The Night Battles: Witchcraft and Agrarian Cults of the 16th and 17th Centuries*, trans. John Tedeschi and Anne Tedeschi. Baltimore, Md.: Johns Hopkins Press.

"Girl Fridays." 1986. *Economist* 301 (Nov. 8): 110.

Gluckman, Max. 1954. *Rituals of Rebellion in South-East Africa*. Manchester: Manchester University Press.

———. 1962. "Les Rites de Passage." Pp. 1–52 in *Essays on the Ritual of Social Relations*, ed. Max Gluckman. Manchester: Manchester University Press.

Gouldner, Alvin W. 1960. "The Norm of Reciprocity: A Preliminary Statement." *American Sociological Review* 25(April): 161–78.

Gramsci, Antonio. 1971. *Selections from the Prison Notebooks*, ed. and trans. Q. Hoare and G. Nowell-Smith. London: Lawrence and Wishart.

Guha, Ranajit, and Gayatri Chakravorty Spivak, eds. 1988. *Selected Subaltern Studies*. New York: Oxford University Press.

Haberman, Clyde. 1986. "For Japan, The Trend Is Dynastic." *New York Times*, July 4, A3.

Hamnett, Ian. 1967. "Ambiguity, Classification and Change: The Function of Riddles." *Man*, n.s. 2(Sept.): 379–92.

Handelman, Don, and Bruce Kapferer. 1980. "Symbolic Types, Mediation and the Transformation of Ritual Context: Sinhalese Demons and Tewa Clowns." *Semiotica* 30(1/2): 41–71.

Havránek, Bohuslaw. 1964. "The Functional Differentiation of the Standard Language." Pp. 3–16 in *A Prague School Reader on Esthetics, Literary Structure and Style*, ed. Paul L. Garvin. Washington, D.C.: Georgetown University Press.

Hayakawa Kōtarō. 1966. *Hanamatsuri* (Flower festival). Tokyo: Iwasaki Bijutsusha.

Hayashiya Tatsusaburō. 1951. "Chayoriai to sono dentō" (Chayoriai [tea party] and its tradition). *Bungaku* 19(May): 34–40.

Hershkowitz, Allen, and Eugene Salerni. 1987. *Garbage Management in Japan: Leading the Way*. New York: INFORM.

Hirano Ryūichi, ed. 1983. *Roppō zensho* (The compendium of Japanese laws). 2 vols. Tokyo: Yūhikaku.

Hobsbawm, Eric J. 1960. *Social Bandits and Primitive Rebels: Studies in Archaic Forms of Social Movement in the 19th and 20th Centuries*. Glencoe, Ill.: Free Press.

Homans, George C. 1950. *The Human Group*. New York: Harcourt, Brace.

———. 1958. "Social Behavior as Exchange." *American Journal of Sociology* 63(May): 597–606.

Hosojima Izumi. 1974. " 'Hadaka no Nihon' no seiji honshitsu—Infure to senkyo to Seirankai to" (Nature of Japanese politics unveiled—Inflation, election, and the Seirankai). *Ekonomisuto* 52(March 25): 142–46.

Hosokawa Ryūgen. 1982. "Nyū rīdā nante hanatare kozō da" (New Leaders? They are just naughty kids). *Gendai* 16(May): 138–45.

Huizinga, Johan. 1952. *Erasmus of Rotterdam*. London: Phaidom Publishers.

———. 1955. *Homo Ludens: A Study of the Play-element in Culture*. Boston: Beacon Press.

Husserl, Edmund. 1967. *Ideas: General Introduction to Pure Phenomenology*. New York: Humanities Press.

Ike, Nobutaka. 1972. *Japanese Politics: Patron-Client Democracy*. 2d ed. New York: Knopf.

———. 1977. "Japanese Political Culture and Democracy." Pp. 378–81 in *Friends, Followers, and Factions*, ed. Steffen W. Schmidt. Berkeley: University of California Press.

Inagami Takeshi. 1974. "Shakai taikei no keikaku riron" (A theory of social system planning). In *Shakaigaku kōza* (Sociology lectures). Pp. 309–44 in vol. 1, *Riron shakaigaku* (Theoretical sociology), ed. Aoi Kazuo. Tokyo: Tokyo Daigaku Shuppankai.

Inose Naoki, Sano Shinichi, and Yamane Isshin. 1978. "Seirankai imada shinazu—Hotto na yabō e ima tosshinchū" (The Seirankai has been by no means dead—Its members are earnestly pursuing their ambition). *Gendai* 12(Oct.): 120–40.

Inoue Hisashi. 1976. "Odōkemono goroshi—Waga Tanaka Kakuei ron," (A killing of trickster—My thoughts on Tanaka Kakuei). *Sekai* 371(Oct.): 122–30.

Inoue Hisashi, Nomoto Kikuo, Suehiro Tamotsu, Betsuyaku Minoru, Matsuda Osamu, Mihashi Osamu, Yamaguchi Masao, Yura Kimiyoshi, and Yokoi Kiyoshi. 1977. *Shinpojiumu—Sabetsu no seishinshi josetsu* (Preface to a spiritual history of discrimination—A symposium). Tokyo: Sanseidō.

Irokawa Daikichi. 1975. "The Survival Struggle of the Japanese Community." *The Japan Interpreter* 9(Spring): 466–94.

Ishida Takeshi. 1961. *Sengo Nihon no seiji taisei* (Postwar Japanese political system). Tokyo: Miraisha.

Ishihara Shintarō. 1974. "Kimi kuni uritamō koto nakare" (Don't you dare betray your country). *Bungei Shunjū* 52(Sept.): 92–106.

Ishii Shinji, ed. 1984. *Gendai shisō nyūmon* (Introduction to modern thoughts). *Takarajima* (special issue) 44.

Ishikawa Masumi. 1973. "Kokkai ni tadayou anun" (A dark cloud is hanging over the Diet). *Asahi Jānaru* 15(30): 7–10.

Itō Shuntarō. 1974. "Kagaku riron hatten no kōzō" (Structure of the development of scientific theory). *Shisō* 595(Jan.): 34–48.

Iwai Tomoaki. 1984. "Kokkai ni okeru seitō no rippō kōdō" (Legislative behavior of political parties in the Diet). In *Nihon no seisaku katei* (Japanese policymaking process), ed. Nakamura Akira and Takeshita Yuzuru. Tokyo: Azusa Shuppansha.

———. 1988. *Rippō katei* (Legislative process). Tokyo: Tokyo Daigaku Shuppankai.

Iwami Takao. 1974. "Ni-Chū kōkūkōshō ga toikakeru mono—Gaikō to seisō to kokueki to" (The questions raised through Sino-Japanese aviation treaty negotiations—Foreign policy, domestic power struggle, and national interest). *Ekonomisuto* 52(May 7) : 22–26.

———. 1977. "Muhabatsu goninotoko no ugoki" (Moves of the five men who belong to no faction). *Chūō Kōron* 92(Jan.): 132–37.

Jakobson, Roman. 1963. *Essais de Linguistigue Générale*. Paris: Éditions de Minuit.

———. 1971. "Two Aspects of Language and Two Types of Aphasic Disturbances." Pp. 67–96 in Roman Jakobson and Morris Halle, *Fundamentals of Language*. 2d ed. The Hague: Mouton.

Jay, Martin. 1971. "How Utopian Is Marcuse?" Pp. 244–56 in *The Revival of American Socialism*, ed. George Fischer. New York: Oxford University Press.

Jiménez, Luz. 1972. *LIfe and Death in Milpa Alta: A Nahuatl Chronicle of Diaz and Zapata*, ed. and trans. Fernando Horcasitas. Norman: University of Oklahoma Press.

"Jimin AA-ken ga shin gurūpu kessei" (LDP Asian-African Studies group formed a new group). 1974. *Ekonomisuto* 52(Feb. 19): 8.

"Jimintōnai ni takamaru Tanaka giin jishokuron" (LDP's domestic public opinion is increasingly for Tanaka's resignation as a Diet member). 1983. *Ekonomisuto* (Oct. 18): 6–7.

"Jimintō tandoku de kokkai saienchō kimeru" (Further extension of the Diet term was decided by the LDP's snap vote). 1973. *Ekonomisuto* 51(Aug. 7): 8.

Jinbo Masahiro. 1978. *Ningen Nakasone Yasuhiro* (Nakasone Yasuhiro as a man). Tokyo: Tōyō Kōronsha.

Jiyū Minshutō (The Liberal Democratic party). 1983. *Tōsoku* (The Liberal Democratic party rule). Tokyo: Jiyū Minshutō.

Jiyū Minshutō Kokkai Taisaku Iinkai (Diet Policy Committee of the Liberal Democratic party). 1970–1983. "Dai 63–100 kokkai—Iinkaibetsu hōritsuan shingi jōkyō" (Processes and results of discussion of bills by committees, from 63d to 100th Diet sessions). Tokyo: Jiyū Minshutō Kokkai Taisaku Iinkai.

"JSP's Decline." 1986. *Daily Yomiuri*, July 9, p. 2.

Jung, C. G. 1969. "On the Psychology of the Trickster Figure," trans. R. F. C. Hull. Pp. 195–211 in Paul Radin, *The Trickster: A Study in American Indian Mythology*. New York: Greenwood Press.

Jyōhō Kenkyūsho, ed. 1983. *Tanaka Kakuei saishin dētashū* (Newest collection of data about Tanaka Kakuei). Tokyo: Kabushikigaisha Dēta Hausu.

Kapferer, Bruce. 1979. "Introduction: Ritual Process and the Transformation of Context." *Social Analysis* 1(Feb.): 3–19.

Karve, Irawati. 1962. "On the Road: A Maharashtrian Pilgrimage." *Asian Studies* (Bombay) 22(Nov.): 13–29.

Kida Minoru [Yamada Yoshihiko]. 1953. *Kiri no buraku* (A hamlet in the fog). Tokyo: Chikuma Shobō.

————. 1957. *Nihon bunka no kontei ni hisomu mono* (The deep core of Japanese culture). Tokyo: Dai Nippon Yūbenkai Kōdansha.

————. 1967. *Nippon buraku* (A Japanese hamlet). Tokyo: Iwanami Shoten.

————. 1981. *Kichigai buraku shūyū kikō* (Ordinary life of a Japanese hamlet called 'Kichigai Buraku' [Crazy Hamlet]). Tokyo: Toyama Shobō.

Kodama Takaya. 1974. "Sabishiki Etsuzankai no jōō: Mōhitotsu no Tanaka Kakueiron" (Lonely queen of the Etsuzankai: Another view of Tanaka Kakuei). *Bungei Shunjū* 52(Nov.): 132–52.

Koike Ryōichi. 1979. "Jimintō saishō kōho 18-nin no kinryoku batsuryoku o kiru" (An inquiry into the financial power and personal networks of the 18 presidential hopefuls of the LDP). *Gendai* 13(Aug.): 106–39.

————. and Group Q. 1980. "Docchiga katsuka Watanabe Michio vs. Nakagawa Ichirō" (Which is going to win, Watanabe Michio or Nakagawa Ichirō?). *Gendai* 14(Sept.): 52–76.

Kojima Kazuo. 1979. *Hōritsu ga dekiru made* (Legislative processes). Tokyo: Gyōsei.

"Kon kokkai o kaerimite" (Looking back to the last Diet session). 1981. *Mineikai Dayori*, no. 2, June 1, p. 3. Newsletter.

Kōsaka Masataka. 1967. "Kyōkō saiketsu no seijigaku" (Politics of the snap vote). *Chūō Kōron* 82(Nov.): 50–69.

Krauss, Ellis S. 1982. "Japanese Parties and Parliament: Changing Leadership Roles and Role Conflict." Pp. 93–114 in *Political Leadership in Contemporary Japan*, ed. Terry Edward MacDougall. Center for Japanese Studies, University of Michigan, Ann Arbor.

————. 1984. "Conflict in the Diet: Toward Conflict Management in Parliamentary Politics." Pp. 243–93 in *Conflict in Japan*, ed. Ellis S. Krauss, Thomas P. Rohlen, and Patricia G. Steinhoff. Honolulu: University of Hawaii Press.

Krauss, Ellis S., Thomas P. Rohlen, and Patricia G. Steinhoff, eds. 1984. *Conflict in Japan*. Honolulu: University of Hawaii Press.

Krupnic, Mark, ed. 1983. *Displacement: Derrida and After*, introduction by Mark Krupnic. Bloomington: Indiana University Press.

Kuhn, Thomas. 1970. *The Structure of Scientific Revolutions*. Chicago: University of Chicago Press.

Kundera, Milan. 1988. "Key Words, Problem Words, Words I Love." *New York Times Book Review*, March 6, pp. 1, 24, 25, 26.

Kuno Chūji. 1988. "Yotō no kokkai unei" (Diet management of the ruling Liberal Democratic party). Pp. 185–200 in *Nihon no kokkai: Shōgen sengo gikaiseiji no ayumi* (The Japanese Diet: Postwar parliamentary politics), ed. Yomiuri Shimbun Chōsa Kenkyū Honbu. Tokyo: Yomiuri Shimbunsha.

Kurimoto Shinichirō. 1979. *Keizai jinruigaku* (Economic Anthropology). Tokyo: Tōyō Keizai Shinpōsha.

———. 1980. *Gensō to shiteno keizai* (Economy as illusion). Tokyo: Seidosha.

———. 1981. *Hō, shakai, shūzoku* (Law, society, and custom). Tokyo: Dōbunkan.

Laclau, Ernesto. 1975. "The Specificity of the Political: The Poulantzas-Miliband Debate," trans. Elizabeth Nash and William Rich. *Economy and Society* 4(Feb.): 87–110.

Leach, Edmund R. 1961a. "Cronus and Chronos." Pp. 124–32 in *Rethinking Anthropology*. London: Athlone Press.

———. 1961b. "Time and False Noses." Pp. 132–36 in *Rethinking Anthropology*. London: Athlone Press.

———. 1964. "Anthropological Aspects of Language: Animal Categories and Verbal Abuse." Pp. 23–63 in *New Directions in the Study of Language*, ed. Eric H. Lenneberg. Cambridge, Mass.: MIT Press.

———. 1967. "Magical Hair." Pp. 77–108 in *Myth and Cosmos: Readings in Mythology and Symbolism*, ed. John Middleton. Garden City, N.Y.: Natural History Press.

———. 1976. *Culture and Communication: The Logic by which Symbols Are Connected*. Cambridge: Cambridge University Press.

Leitch, Vincent B. 1983. *Deconstructive Criticism: An Advanced Introduction*. New York: Columbia University Press.

Lévi-Strauss, Claude. 1963. "The Structural Study of Myth." Pp. 206–31 in *Structural Anthropology*, trans. Claire Jacobson and Brooke Grundfest Schoepf. New York: Basic Books.

———. 1966. *The Savage Mind*. Chicago: University of Chicago Press.

Lipton, Lawrence. 1959. *The Holy Barbarians*. New York: Messner.

Lukes, Steven. 1974. *Power: A Radical View*. London: Macmillan.

———. 1977. *Essays in Social Theory*. New York: Columbia University Press.

McGlashan, Alan. 1967. *The Savage and Beautiful Country*. Boston: Houghton Mifflin.

McLuhan, Marshall. 1964. *Understanding Media: The Extensions of Man*. New York: McGraw-Hill.

Mailer, Norman. 1959. *Advertisement of Myself*. New York: Putnam.

Mainichi Shimbunsha. 1983. "Nagatachō no urakanshū" (Informal customs in Nagatachō). A portion of the special feature series, "Kinken" (Money politics). *Mainichi Shimbun*, Aug. 25–31, Nos. 29–35.

Malcolm X. 1966. *The Autobiography of Malcolm X*. New York: Grove.

Mannheim, Karl. 1936. *Ideology and Utopia: An Introduction to the Sociology of Knowledge*. New York: Harcourt Brace Jovanovich.

Marcuse, Herbert. 1966. *Eros and Civilization: A Philosophical Inquiry into Freud*. Boston: Beacon Press.

————. 1969. *An Essay on Liberation*. Boston: Beacon Press.

————. 1972. *Counterrevolution and Revolt*. Boston: Beacon Press.

————. 1978. *The Aesthetic Dimension: Toward a Critique of Marxist Aesthetics*. Boston: Beacon Press.

Marx, Karl. 1964. *Karl Marx: Early Writings*, ed. and trans. T. B. Bottomore. New York: McGraw-Hill.

Massey, Joseph A. 1975. "The Missing Leader: Japanese Youth's view of Political Authority." *American Political Science Review* 69(March): 31–48.

Matsumoto Shirō. 1983. "Tanakaha wa ijō bōchō buttai de aru" (The Tanaka faction is an extraordinary, expansionist creature). *Bungei Shunjū* 61(March): 114–24.

Matsuo Yōichi. 1986. " 'Takeshi genshō' o kangaeru—Gendai ni okeru warai no tokushitsu" (The 'Takeshi phenomenon'—An analysis of the characteristic of laughter in modern society). *Sekai* 494(Nov.): 37–44.

Matsushita Keiichi. 1962. *Gendai Nihon no seijiteki kōsei* (Organization of modern Japanese politics). Tokyo: Tokyo Daigaku Shuppankai.

Meyer, Robert R. 1972. *Social Planning and Social Change*. Englewood Cliffs, N.J.: Prentice-Hall.

Miliband, Ralph. 1969. *The State in Capitalist Society*. London: Weidenfeld and Nicolson.

————. 1970. "The Capitalist State: Reply to Nicos Poulantzas." *New Left Review* 59(Jan./Feb.): 53–60.

Minato Tetsurō, and the Seirankai. 1974. *Seirankai kara no chokugen* (Direct words from the Seirankai). Tokyo: Rōman.

Miyagawa Takayoshi, ed. 1980. *Seiji handobukku* (Political handbook). Tokyo: Seiji Kōhō Sentā.

Miyagi Otoya. 1982. "Tanaka Kakuei no seikaku" (Nature and characteristics of Tanaka Kakuei). Pp. 16–53 in Miyagi Otoya, Oda Susumu, Miyagawa Takayoshi, Okano Kaoru, Kase Hideaki, Bernard Krisher, and Andrew Horvart, *Tanaka Kakuei to Nihonjin* (Tanaka Kakuei and the Japanese). Tokyo: Yamate Shobō.

Mochizuki, Mike. 1982. "Managing and Influencing the Japanese Legislative Process: The Role of Parties and the National Diet." Ph.D. diss., Harvard University, Cambridge.

Moore, Sally Falk, and Barbara G. Myerhoff, eds. 1975. *Symbol and Politics in Communal Ideology: Cases and Questions*. Ithaca, N.Y.: Cornell University Press.

Mouer, Ross, and Yoshio Sugimoto. 1986. *Images of Japanese Society: A Study in the Structure of Sociological Reality*. London: KPI.

Murakawa Ichirō. 1985. *Nihon no seisaku kettei katei* (The Japanese policymaking process). Tokyo: Gyōsei.

Murobushi Tetsurō. 1981. *Oshoku no kōzō* (The structure of corruption). Tokyo: Iwanami Shoten.

Myerhoff, Barbara, and Jay Ruby. 1982. "Introduction." Pp. 1–35 in *A Crack in the Mirror: Reflexive Perspectives in Anthropology*, ed. Jay Ruby. Philadelphia: University of Pennsylvania Press.

Nagata Tarō. 1983. "Yatō baishūhi 30-oku en o nigiru kokkai taisaku iin no kenbō jutsusū" (Intrigue of the LDP Diet Policy Committee members who keep as much as 3 billion yen for the bribery of the opposition). *Seikai Ōrai* 49(Dec.): 42–53.

Naitō Kunio. 1981. "Nakagawa Ichirō—Ichido wa yaritai Bōeichō chōkan" (An interview with Nakagawa Ichirō—I wish I could be a director-general of the Defense Agency once in a lifetime). *Gendai* 15(March): 242–56.

Nakada Akira. 1983. "Seijika to namida" (Politician and tears). *Mainichi Shimbun*, Nov. 3, p. 5.

Nakagawa Ichirō. 1979. "Nakagawa Ichirō, Jimintō, zōzei, enerugī o kiru" (Nakagawa Ichirō critically comments on the Liberal Democratic party, tax increase issue, and energy problem). Interview by *Gendai*. *Gendai* 13(Oct.): 90–100.

Nakagawa Yatsuhiro. 1979. "Japan, the welfare superpower." *Journal of Japanese Studies* 5(1979): 5–51.

Nakamura Kikuo. 1974. "The 'Japanese' in 'Japanese Politics,' " trans. Ross Mouer. *Keiō Journal of Politics* 1(Spring): 1–17.

Nakane Chie. 1970. *Japanese Society*. London: Weidenfeld and Nicolson.

Nakano Shiro. 1981. "Nakagawa Ichirō—'Honryū' o sekitome isseihōki no arashi o yobutoki" (Nakagawa Ichirō—Now is the time to rebel against the mainstream of the party). *Gendai* 15(June): 61–65.

" 'Nakisone-san' namida no isseki—Sokuin no jō, dōri hikkomu" (Nakasone talked in tears—His sympathy and compassion let emotion overpower reason at the gathering). *Mainichi Shimbun*, Nov. 1, 1983, evening edition.

Natanson, Maurice A. 1962a. "Knowledge and Alienation: Some Remarks on Mannheim's Sociology of Knowledge." Pp. 167–71 in *Literature, Philosophy, and the Social Sciences: Essays in Existentialism and Phenomenology*. The Hague: Martinus Nijhoff.

———. 1962b. "Phenomenology: A Viewing." Pp. 3–25 in *Literature, Philosophy, and the Social Sciences: Essays in Existentialism and Phenomenology*. The Hague: Martinus Nijhoff.

Newfield, Jack. 1966. *A Prophetic Minority: The American New Left*. London: Anthony Blond.

Nihon Seikei Shimbunsha. 1956–1986. *Kokkai binran* (Diet handbook). Tokyo: Nihon Seikei Shimbunsha.

Nishigaki Seiji. 1977. *Kamigami to minshū undō* (Gods and ordinary people's movements). Tokyo: Mainichi Shimbunsha.

Noguchi Hiroshi. 1973. *Katasutorofī no riron* (Theory of catastrophe). Tokyo: Kōdansha.

Oda Makoto, ed. 1969. *Jiritsu suru shimin* (Citizens are now getting independent). Tokyo: Asahi Shimbunsha.

Oda Susumu. 1982. "Seijiteki minwa to shite no 'Tanaka Kakuei' genshō" (The Takana Kakuei phenomenon as political folklore). Pp. 55–76 in Miyagi Otoya et al., *Tanaka Kakuei to Nihonjin* (Tanaka Kakuei and the Japanese). Tokyo: Yamate Shobō.

Ohnuki-Tierney, Emiko. 1984. *Illness and Culture in Contemporary Japan: An Anthropological View*. New York: Cambridge University Press.

———. 1990. "Monkey as Metaphor? Transformations of a Polytropic Symbol in Japanese Culture." *Man*, n.s., 25(1)(March): 89–107.

"Onkō iinchō ni furute iraira" (Veteran Diet members are irritated by a committee chairman who is inefficient in personal relations). *Asahi Shimbun*, Feb. 14, 1984.

Oriental Wave. 1982–1984. Nos. 1–5. Tokyo: LDP Representative Watanuki Tamisuke Office, Minpōkai.

Ōtake Hideo. 1983. "Sengo hoshu taisei no tairitsujiku" (Contending two poles in the post-war conservative regime). *Chūō Kōron* 98(April): 137–51.

Packard, George R. III. 1966. *Protest in Tokyo: The Security Treaty Crisis of 1960*. Princeton, N.J.: Princeton University Press.

Pareles, Jon. 1990. "Rap: Slick, Violent, Nasty and Maybe, Hopeful." *New York Times*, June 17, E1, E5.

Parsons, Talcott. 1951. *The Social System*. Glencoe, Ill.: Free Press.

Pempel, T. J. 1974. "The Bureaucratization of Policymaking in Postwar Japan." *American Journal of Political Science* 18(Nov.): 647–64.

———. 1982. *Policy and Politics in Japan: Creative Conservatism*. Philadelphia: Temple University Press.

Plath, David W. 1964. *The After Hours: Modern Japan and the Search for Enjoyment*. Berkeley: University of California Press.

Polanyi, Karl. 1966. *Dahomey and the Slave Trade*. Seattle: University of Washington Press.

Polanyi, Karl, Conrad M. Arensberg, and Harry W. Pearson, eds. 1957. *Trade and Market in the Early Empires: Economies in History and Theory*. Glencoe, Ill.: Free Press.

Popper, Karl. 1959. *The Logic of Scientific Discovery*. London: Hutchinson.

———. 1970. "Normal Science and Its Dangers." In *Criticism and the Growth of Knowledge*, ed. I. Lakatos and A. Musgrave. New York: Cambridge University Press.

Poulantzas, Nicos. 1969. "The Problem of the Capitalist State." *New Left Review* 58(Nov./Dec.): 67–78.

———. 1973. *Political Power and Social Class*, ed. and trans. Timothy O'Hagan. London: New Left Books (NLB); Sheed and Ward.

Radin, Paul. 1969. *The Trickster: A Study in American Indian Mythology*. New York: Greenwood Press.

"Rankiryū no naka no Jimintō" (LDP in the midst of turbulent air). 1974. *Sekai* 341(April): 186–89.

Rappaport, Roy A. 1980. "Concluding Comments on Ritual and Reflexivity." *Semiotica* 30(1/2): 181–93.

"The Razor-Blade Oath." 1973. *Newsweek*, July 30, 37.

Ryan, Michael. 1983. "Deconstruction and Social Theory: The Case of Liberalism." Pp. 154–68 in *Displacemant: Derrida and After*, ed. Mark Krupinck. Bloomington: Indiana University Press.

Sahlins, Marshall D. 1976. *Culture and Practical Reason*. Chicago: University of Chicago Press.

———. 1981. "The Stranger-King: Or Dumezil among the Fijians." *Journal of Pacific History* 16(July): 107–32.

———. 1983. "Other Times, Other Customs: The Anthropology of History." *American Anthropologist* 85 (Sept.): 517–44.

Saitō Eizaburō. 1983. *Saishō Nakasone Yasuhiro no shisō to kōdō* (Thoughts and activities of Prime Minister Nakasone Yasuhiro). Tokyo: Nihon Keizai Tsūshinsha.

Sasaki Yoshitaka. 1983a. "Nakasone, Tanaka no antō no sue ni hashiri dashita shūin '11-gatsu kaisan,' " (The political situation has started moving toward 'November election' after under-the-surface struggles between Nakasone and Tanaka). *Shūkan Asahi* (Nov.4): 175–77.

———. 1983b. "Zenjitsu ni shōbu ga tsuite ita Tanakasone kaidan no kōbō," (A revelation of the secret midday meeting—The result has already been decided in the previous day of the Tanaka-Nakasone meeting). *Shūkan Asahi* (Nov. 11): 20–24.

Satō Seizaburō and Matsuzaki Tetsuhisa. 1986. *Jimintō seiken* (The Liberal Democratic party government). Tokyo: Chūō Kōronsha.

Saussure, Ferdinand de. 1966. *Course in General Linguistics*, ed. Charles Balley and Albert Sechehaye; trans. with an intro. and notes, Wade Baskin. New York: McGraw-Hill.

Sawa Takamitsu, and Ushiki Shigehiro. 1975 "Shitsuteki genshō no kaiseki-gaku: Katasutorofī no riron to shakai ninshiki" (An analysis of the phenomenon of qualitative change: Theory of catastrophe and social cognition). *Shisō* 613(July): 17–36.

Scalapino, Robert A., and Junnosuke Masumi. 1962. *Parties and Politics in Contemporary Japan*. Berkeley: University of California Press.

Schiller, Freidrich. 1965. *On the Aesthetic Education of Man: In a Series of Letters*, trans. with an intro., Reginald Snell. New York: Frederick Ungar Publishing.

Schmidt, Steffen W., ed. 1977. *Friends, Followers, and Factions*. Berkeley: University of California Press.

Schutz, Alfred. 1944. "The Stranger: An Essay in Social Psychology." *American Journal of Sociology* 49(May): 499–507.

———. 1970. *Alfred Schutz on Phenomenology and Social Relations: Selected Writings*, ed. Helmut R. Wagner. Chicago: University of Chicago Press.

Scott, James C. 1989. "Everyday Forms of Resistance." Pp. 3–33 in *Everyday Forms of Peasant Resistance*, ed. Forrest D. Colburn. New York: M. E. Sharpe.

Secretariat, House of Representatives. 1982. *The National Diet of Japan: The Constitution of Japan, Diet Law, The Rules of House of Representatives*. Tokyo: Secretariat, House of Representatives.

"Seirankai to Tanaka naikaku to" (The Seirankai and the Tanaka Cabinet). 1974. *Ekonomisuto* 52(Feb. 5): 44.

Seymour-Ure, Colin. 1974. "Private Eye: The Politics of the Fool." Pp. 240–83 in *The Political Impact of Mass Media*. London: Constable; Beverly Hills, Calif.: Sage Publications.

Shepperson, George, and Thomas Price. 1958. *Independent African: John Chilembwe and the Origins, Setting and Significance of the Nyasaland Native Rising of 1915*. Edinburgh: Edinburgh University Press.

Shiibashi Katsunobu. 1982. "Nyū rīdā Abe, Nakagawa no kenkyū" (A study of new leaders, Abe and Nakagawa). *Ekonomisuto* 60(Nov. 30): 34–39.

Shiina Etsusaburō Tsuitōroku Kankōkai. 1982. *Shiina Etsusaburō shashinshū* (Reminiscent pictures of the late Shiina Etsusaburō). Tokyo: Shiina Etsusaburō Tsuitōroku Kankōkai.

Shils, Edward, ed. 1975. *Center and Periphery: Essay in Macrosociology*. Chicago: University of Chicago Press.

Shiota Michihiko, and Magami Hiroshi. 1980. "Hamada Kōichi kakute tōsensu" (Hamada Kōichi has thus won the elections). *Bungei Shunjū* 58(June): 126–44.

Shūgiin Jimukyoku. 1981–1982. *Dai 94–95 (1980–81) Shūgiin iinkai giroku (Ōkura)* (The 94th-95th Diet proceedings of the House of Representatives committees: Finance committee). Tokyo: Ōkurashō Insatsukyoku.

Simmel, Georg. 1950. *The Sociology of Georg Simmel*, trans., ed., and intro., Kurt H. Wolff. Glencoe, Ill.: Free Press.

"Sonohi no Tanaka Kakuei, 1983, 10.12" (Tanaka Kakuei, on the day, October 12, 1983). 1983. *Asahi Jānaru* (Oct. 21): 12–15.

Stonequist, Everett V. 1937. *The Marginal Man: A Study in Personality and Culture Conflict*. New York: C. Scribner's Sons.

Suzuki Tsuneo. 1976. "Nakasone Yasuhiroron" (On Nakasone Yasuhiro). *Ekonomisuto* 54(Aug. 24): 22–26.

Tachibana Takashi. 1974. "Tanaka Kakuei—Sono kinmyaku to jinmyaku—" (A study of Tanaka Kakuei—Basis of his financial power and his personal networks). *Bungei Shunjū* 52(Nov.): 92–131.

———. 1976. *Tanaka Kakuei kenkyū* (A study of Tanaka Kakuei). 2 vols. Tokyo: Kōdansha.

Takeda Seiji, and Nagasawa Tetsu. 1984. "Kōzōshugi kara posutokōzōshugi e" (From structuralism to poststructuralism). *Takarajima* (special issue) 44:189–224.

"Tanaka jishoku, 'Jō de unagashita' " (Nakasone "induced" Tanaka to resign "with emotion"). 1983. *Yomiuri Shimbun*, Nov. 1, p. 1 (evening issue).

Tanaka Kakuei. 1972. *Watakushi no rirekisho* (My personal history). Tokyo: Nihon Keizai Shimbunsha.

———. 1973. *Jiden watakushi no shōnen jidai* (Autobiography—My younger years). Tokyo: Kōdansha.

Tanaka Zenichirō. 1981. *Jimintō taisei no seiji shidō* (Ruling of the LDP-centered political system). Tokyo: Daiichi Hōki Shuppan.

Tawara Sōichirō. 1978a. "Fukuda Takeo no ōgon no hibi" (Golden days of Fukuda Takeo). *Chūō Kōron* 93(Nov.): 174–98.

——. 1978b. "Seirankai maboroshi no hanran" (Unrealized rebellion of the Seirankai). *Chūō Kōron* 93(Dec.): 172–86.

——. 1983. "Shōsetsu Nakagawa Ichirō" (Nakagawa Ichirō story). *Shōsetsu Gendai* 21(April): 56–73.

Thayer, Nathaniel B. 1969. *How the Conservatives Rule Japan.* Princeton, N.J.: Princeton University Press.

Thom, René. 1975. *Structural Stability and Morphogenesis: An Outline of a General Theory of Models*, trans. D. H. Fowler. Reading, Mass.: W. A. Benjamin.

Thompson, Michael. 1979. *Rubbish Theory: The Creation and Destruction of Value.* Oxford: Oxford University Press.

Tocqueville, Alexis de. 1955. *Democracy in America.* 2 vols. New York: Vintage Books.

Togawa Isamu. 1980. *Kimi wa Tanaka Kakuei ni nareruka* (If you could become a Tanaka Kakuei). Tokyo: Yamate Shobō.

——. 1980–81. *Shōsetsu Yoshida gakkō* (The Yoshida School). 8 vols. Tokyo: Kadokawa Shoten.

——. 1982. *Nagatachō no tōsō* (Power struggles in Nagatachō). 2 vols. Tokyo: Mainichi shimbunsha.

"Tokyo-hatsu Peking bin no yukue" (A destination of Tokyo flight bound for Beijing). 1974. *Ekonomisuto* 52(April 16): 19.

Tominaga Kenichi. 1965. *Shakai hendō no riron* (Theory of social dynamics). Tokyo: Iwanami Shoten.

——. 1973. "Shakai taikei bunseki to shakai keikakuron" (An analysis of social system and social planning theory). *Shisō* 587(May): 51–66.

Tominomori Eiji. 1974. "Ushinawareta jūkōzō" (Flexibility of the LDP's decision-making structure has been lost). *Sekai* 346(Sept.): 239–44.

Trotsky, Leon. 1969. *The Permanent Revolution, and the Results and Prospects.* New York: Merit Publishers.

Turner, Terrence. 1977. "Transformation, Hierarchy and Transcendence: A Reformulation of Van Gennep's Model of the Structure of Rites de Passage." Pp. 53–70 in Sally F. Moore and Barbara G. Myerhoff, eds. *Secular Ritual* Assen: Van Gorcum.

Turner, Victor W. 1968. "Myth and Symbol" Pp. 576–82 in *International Encyclopedia of the Social Sciences*, ed. David L. Sills. Vol. 10. New York: Macmillan; Free Press.

——. 1974. *Dramas, Fields, and Metaphors: Symbolic Action in Human Society.* Ithaca, N.Y.: Cornell University Press.

——. 1977. *The Ritual Process: Structure and Anti-Structure.* Ithaca, N.Y.: Cornell University Press.

Ueno Chizuko. 1977. "Kaosu, kosumosu, nomosu" (Chaos, cosmos, and nomos). *Shisō* 640(Oct.): 101–22.

——. 1981. "Kōkan no kōdo, kenryoku no kōdo—Kigōron to keizaigaku"

(Code of exchange, code of power—Semiotics and economics). *Keizai Hyōron* 30(Oct.): 98–113.

Utsumi Hideo, Kusunoki Masatoshi, Nakagawa Ichirō, Morishita Motoharu, Watanabe Michio, Kimura Takeo, and Shioguchi Kiichi. 1973. "Daijin kokoroe de dō kawaru—Seirankai jikan no 'yūkoku no shijō'" (How the Seirankai's "Patriotic zeal" would change after its five members took posts of vice-minister [five] at a time). *Shūkan Asahi* 78(Dec. 14): 18–23.

Van Gennep, Arnold. 1960. *The Rites of Passage*, trans. Monika B. Vizedom and Gabrielle L. Caffee. London: Routledge and Kegan Paul.

Wakamori Tarō. 1944. "Chūsei ni okeru kyōdōtai no chitsujo to jinja" (Community order and Shinto shrine in the Middle Ages). *Shakai Keizai Shigaku* 13(4): 309–44.

Watanabe Sumio. 1945. "Chūsei shaji o chūshin to seru rakusho kishō ni tsuite" (A study of written oaths and other materials of the Middle Ages found in the Buddhist temples and Shinto shrines). *Shigaku Zasshi* 56(March): 73–106.

Watanabe Tsuneo. 1974. "'Seirankai' o ronzu" (On Seirankai). *Bungei Shunjū* 52(July): 92–103.

Weller, Robert. 1986. "Where Village Chiefs Still Hold Sway." *Daily Yomiuri*, April 28, p. 5.

Welsford, Enid. 1935. *The Fool: His Social and Literary History*. London: Faber and Faber.

Wescott, Joan. 1962. "The Sculpture and Myths of Eshu-Elegba, the Yoruba Trickster." *Africa* 32(Oct.): 336–54.

Willeford, William. 1969. *The Fool and His Scepter: A Study of Clowns and Jesters and Their Audience*. London: E. Arnold.

Williams, Gwyn A. 1960. "The Concept of 'Egemonia' in the Thought of Antonio Gramsci: Some Notes on Interpretation." *Journal of the History of Ideas* 21(4): 586–99.

Wolff, Kurt H., and Barrington Moore, eds. 1967. *The Critical Spirit: Essays in Honor of Herbert Marcuse*. Boston: Beacon Press.

Yamaguchi Masao. 1969. "Bunka to kyōki" (Culture and Madness). *Chūō Kōron* 84(Jan.): 337–57.

———. 1974. "La royauté et le Symbolisme Dualiste chez les Jukun de Nigeria." *Journal of Asian and African Studies* 8(1974): 1–30.

———. 1975. *Bunka to ryōgisei* (Culture and ambiguity) Tokyo: Iwanami Shoten.

———. 1977a. "Bunka kigōron kenkyū ni okeru 'ika' no gainen" (The applicability of the concept of "ostranenie" in the study of culture in anthropology). *Shisō* 640(Oct.): 40–59.

———. 1977b. "Kingship, Theatricality, and Marginal Reality in Japan." Pp. 151–79 in *Text and Context: The Social Anthropology of Tradition*, ed. Ravindra K. Jain. Philadelphia: Institute for the Study of Human Issues.

Yamamoto Kōichi. 1988. "Yatō no kokkai tōsō" ("The opposition parties' Diet struggle." Pp. 159–84 in *Nihon no kokkai: Shōgen sengo gikaiseiji no ayumi* (The

Japanese Diet: Postwar parliamentary politics), ed. Yomiuri Shimbun Chōsa Kenkyū Honbu. Tokyo: Yomiuri Shimbunsha.

Yamashita Katsutoshi. 1974. "Abarenbō Seirankai ni taikō suru Jimintō hatoha no 'oie no jijō' " (Private reasons of the LDP doves who are fighting with rowdy Seirankai members). *Shūkan Asahi* 79(Feb. 22): 130–32.

"Yasukuni Jinja to Ni-Chū kōkūkōro no aida" (Between the Yasukuni Shrine issue and Sino-Japanese aviation treaty negotiations). 1974. *Ekonomisuto* 52(April 30): 25.

Yokoi Kiyoshi. 1975. *Chūsei minshū no seikatsu bunka* (Life and culture of ordinary people of the Middle Ages). Tokyo: Tokyo Daigaku Shuppankai.

Yokoi Kiyoshi, Amino Yoshihiko, Abe Kinya, Chiba Tokuji, Noji Kōji, Sakashita Keihachi, Moriya Tsuyoshi. 1986. "Akutō to tsubute/Warabe to asobi" (Akutō [a villain] and a stone/Children and play). In *Shūkan Asahi Hyakka: Nihon no Rekishi*, vol. 4, no. 10. Tokyo: Asahi Shimbunsha.

Yoshimura Tadashi. 1964. *Nihon seiji no shindan* (A diagnosis of Japanese politics). Tokyo: Seishin Shobō.

INDEX

ambiguities, xii, 12–13, 15, 35, 42, 61, 76, 101, 110, 115–16

blood oath, 90–91, 95, 97, 99, 110
board of directors, 33, 36–38, 42

catastrophe, 24, 61–62, 106, 111, 118, 121
chaos, xi–xii, xiv, 6, 8, 12–13, 20–21, 55, 93, 100, 102, 106, 108, 113–15, 117–18
charisma, 101–2
comedians, 57, 59, 85, 110
communitas, 10–11, 18–20, 53, 55, 117. See also *structure*
cosmos, xi–xii, xiv, 8–9, 12, 15, 20–22, 55, 98, 100, 106, 109–10, 114–15, 117–18

deformation, 14–15, 22–23, 42, 78, 100, 102
deformer, 13, 23, 59, 61, 77, 101, 103, 110, 115
democracy, 5, 25, 110, 116, 118–21
democratic ideology, 112, 120
democratic political arrangements, 113, 116
dereifying function, xiv, 110. *See also* reflexivity; reifying force
dualism, 47, 77, 101

ecstasy, 9
ecstatic collective activities, 115
election campaign, 23, 26, 44–45, 47–59, 110

Finance Committee, 23, 26, 29, 31, 36–37, 110. *See also* Watanuki Committee
Fools, 61, 85
freedom, 5, 25, 116–17

individualism, 25, 119–21

laughter, xiii, 17, 24, 59, 111
liminal experiences, xiii–xiv, 23, 26, 32, 39, 41, 43, 56, 101, 115. *See also* symbolic experiences
liminal state, xii–xiv, 11–17, 21–24, 26, 61, 75–76, 78, 101–2, 110–18, 121

liminality, xiii, 11–12, 14–16, 24, 27, 47, 77–78, 101–3, 106. *See also* marginality
Lockheed bribery case, 62–63, 70, 72, 83

marginal beings, xii–xiv, 11–16, 21–22, 24, 26, 77–78, 84, 101, 110–18, 121
marginality, xi, 3, 9, 11, 80, 85, 99. *See also* liminality
marginal/liminal domain, xii, 20–22, 25–26, 114; intrusion of, 42, 44, 56. *See also* symbolic dimension; symbolic intrusion
metaphor, 18–20, 22, 75
metonymy, 18–20, 22, 75

Nakagawa Ichirō, 78–89, 91–92, 94–97, 101, 106
Nakasone Yasuhiro, 61–75, 78, 87, 101–2, 106–9, 111
nomos, xi–xiv, 8, 10, 12–13, 15–17, 20–22, 24, 35, 39, 41–42, 45, 55, 59, 61, 74–77, 84, 95, 98, 100–102, 105, 107, 109–18

play, xiii, 23–24, 60–61, 111, 116
power, xiii–xiv, 4–6, 25, 116, 119, 121; and change, xi, 101; concept of, xiv, 4–5, 116–17; nature of, xi; of ordinary people, 16
purity, 49, 99, 107

reflexive consciousness, 116. *See also* reified consciousness
reflexivity, xii–xiv, 11–12, 15, 17, 22, 24, 45, 48, 56, 59–60, 77–78, 110–13, 115–16, 121. *See also* dereifying function; reification; reified consciousness
reification, xiii, 9–10, 15, 85, 116, 121. *See also* reflexivity
reified consciousness, 113, 116, 120. *See also* reflexive consciousness; reflexivity
reifying force, 5, 111–12, 114, 116, 121. *See also* dereifying function
ritual exchange, 45–48
ritual symbolism, xiii

sacred order, 9